The Formless Self

The Formless Self

Joan Stambaugh

State University of New York Press

Published by
State University of New York Press, Albany

© 1999 State University of New York

For information, address State University of New York Press,
State University Plaza, Albany, N.Y., 12246

Production by Dale Cotton
Marketing by Nancy Farrell

Library of Congress Cataloging-in-Publication Data

Stambaugh, Joan, 1932–
    The formless self / Joan Stambaugh.
        p.   cm.
    Includes index.
    ISBN 0–7914–4149–0 (hardcover : alk. paper). — ISBN 0–7914–4150–4
(pbk. : alk. paper)
    1. Self (Philosophy)   2. Philosophy, Japanese.   3. Religion—
Philosophy.   4. Dōgen, 1200–1253.   5. Hisamatsu, Shin'ichi,
1894–1976.   6. Nishitani, Keiji, 1900–1990.   I. Title.
B5243.S44S73   1999
126'.0952—dc21   98–27672
                                                          CIP

10 9 8 7 6 5 4 3 2 1

For Roy Finch

Contents

Property was thus appall'd
That the self was not the same;
Single nature's double name
Neither two nor one was call'd.

Reason, in itself confounded,
Saw division grow together;
To themselves yet either neither
Simple were so well compounded,

That it cried, 'How true a twain
Seemeth this concordant one!
Love hath reason, reason none,
If what parts can so remain.

From "The Phoenix and the Turtle"
                    Shakespeare

$$\overbrace{\quad\textit{Preface}\quad}$$

This study attempts to probe into the meaning of the self as set forth by three Japanese Buddhist thinkers: Dōgen, Hisamatsu, and Nishitani. Dōgen lived in the thirteenth century—Hisamatsu and Nishitani in the twentieth.

Dōgen's main work, Shōbōgenzō, *Treasury of the True Dharma Eye*, has received considerable attention and may be considered one of the most profound and challenging philosophical works of Buddhism in any period. Hisamatsu is perhaps less well known in the West; his main work in English is *Zen and the Fine Arts*. In addition, he has authored some articles available in English, most notably "The Characteristics of Oriental Nothingness" and the dialogues with the Protestant theologian Paul Tillich. Nishitani engaged in extensive studies of Western philosophy and religion; the book *Religion and Nothingness* is his attempt to put Buddhist concepts in a form also accessible to Western thinkers.

What these three thinkers have in common is, among other things, a concern with the problem of the self. Formulated by Hisamatsu as the Formless Self, the resultant concept of self develops in a way that merges self and world with a total lack of objectification or reification of either.

In this work, I have tried to pursue some questions raised in my earlier book, *Impermanence is Buddha-nature*. That work centered almost exclusively on Dōgen and the question of time. This study again is concerned with Dōgen and then goes beyond the thirteenth century to consider a less well-known Buddhist thinker, Shin'ichi Hisamatsu, in his own essays as well as in dialogues with the Protestant theologian Paul Tillich. Finally, attention is focused on Keiji Nishitani, a Buddhist scholar who devoted himself to the study of Western philosophy and theology. Thus, the far-reaching implications of impermanence for the question of the self are pursued in an attempt to reach an understanding of nonsubstantialized self that has nothing to do with a reified ego.

This can hardly claim to be the work of a scholar of Buddhism. The only credentials the author can lay claim to are some years of Sanskrit study, an all too short period of study with the German scholar of Indology and Buddhism, Erich Frauwallner, as well as an equally short period of study with Masao Abe, plus a lifelong keen interest in the East and in Buddhism in particular. However, the limitations in comprehension are decidedly my own and no one else's responsibility.

This study is an attempt to present Eastern ideas, or at least one Western interpretation of Eastern ideas, to Western readers in a meaningful way. Now that philosophers have to a large extent exhausted their fascination with substantialist metaphysics, the opportunity to explore Buddhist thoughts may be welcome.

One of the many Buddhist names for ultimate reality is the Form-less Self. The term "self" is not without its problems in the context of Buddhist thought. One of the few utterances traceable to the Buddha himself involves the statement that all things are without self. Early Buddhism (*Theravada, Hinayana*) was exceedingly concerned with uprooting this firmly entrenched and much cherished view of the self that we cling to so tenaciously. That view of the self is inextricably bound up with the Buddha's two other statements that all things are suffering and all things are impermanent. We ultimately "suffer" because there is no such thing as a permanently enduring self. In fact, one of the lasting insights of the Buddha is that there is no enduring self in anyone or anything at all.

On the other hand, a perhaps even more fundamental and comprehensive utterance traceable to the Buddha is that we must at all costs avoid the two extremes of permanence (*sasvata*) and nihilism (*uccheda*). We all want to be able to say either that there is a permanent self or an immortal soul or else that there is nothing at all but physiology, nerves, ganglia, blood and so forth, destined to rot in the ground to which they are eventually entrusted. But anyone making either of these two statements is, according to the Buddha, simply dead wrong. So there is no neat conceptual answer to this supreme existential question of the self. But there are many fruitful indicators pointing the way to a soteriological, not a conceptual, "solution"/"answer."

Most thinking people, not just the philosophers, have always been concerned with the question of the self, with the question of who they are—of the reality of who or what they are. This is natural, inevitable, and perfectly wholesome. A problem arises when the emphasis comes exclusively to focus, not on the *reality* of who they are, but on the reality of who *they* are, of who *I* am. Then, to employ a useful distinction made by C. G. Jung and others, the self, an initially neutral term, becomes the ego, a term implying blind and insistent preoccupation with *my* self accompanied by a determined rejection of any other reality at all costs.

But the true search is not just for my self which then tends to degenerate into narcissistic ego-infatuation, but for *reality*, whatever that may be. And reality is going to lie beyond the dimension of the ego without therefore necessarily being anything transcendent. This study attempts to probe into whatever some Buddhists meant by the somewhat enigmatic phrase: The Formless Self. The study will concentrate selectively on aspects of Dōgen, Hisamatsu, and Nishitani.

Dōgen

The Question of the Self

Perhaps the clearest access to the question of the self in Dōgen lies in the fascicle of Shōbōgenzō entitled *"Genjō-kōan."* Because all issues are so intimately and inextricably interwoven in Dōgen's thought, it is difficult and even artificial to isolate one question from all the rest. Yet we must choose the most direct inroad available to us to the question of the self.

> To study the Buddha-way is to study the self; to study the self is to forget the self; to forget the self is to be verified by myriad dharmas; and to be verified by myriad dharmas is to drop off the body-mind of the self as well as the body-mind of the other. There remains no trace of enlightenment, and one lets this traceless enlightenment come forth for ever and ever.[1]

If one wishes to study the Buddha-way, the only place to start, the only initial access, is one's own self; one cannot search for it somewhere outside the self. When one studies the self, really studies the self, one does not encounter an enduring substantial thing called "self." What, then, does one encounter? One encounters the myriad dharmas, the ten thousand things of the world and thereby forgets the self that one did not find. These myriad dharmas verify and confirm one's activity and this allows body-mind to drop off. When one's body-mind drops off, the notion of the body-mind of the other drops off as well. Dropping off body-mind (*Shinjin datsuraku*) allows the transparency of enlightenment to enter. Enlightenment leaves no trace, as this would imply a dualism between the dropped off body-mind and enlightenment. This traceless enlightenment, absolutely free from any kind of dualism whatsoever, is then free to come forth and continue for ever and ever.

Only when the self gives way to allow the myriad dharmas to enter, does the self become what it truly is. Its true function is to become utterly transparent to the myriad things of the world, be they other people, realities of nature, man-made things or whatever. In the words of D. T. Suzuki:

> It is the Heart indeed that tells us that our own self is a self only to the extent that it disappears into all other selves, non-sentient as well as sentient.[2]

The self is never some kind of substantial object, something over against us that we can find. In his *Traktatus Logico-Philosophicus*, Ludwig Wittgenstein illustrated this graphically by drawing a picture of the eye and stating that this is not what we see when we look.[3] The eye (or the self) is at best that with which we see; it is never *what* we see. Jean-Paul Sartre, in a totally different context, and from a totally different perspective, stated pretty much the same thing in *The Transcendence of the Ego*. What we get is always the me, the object, never the I, the subject or self.

Going back to the beginning of *Genjō-kōan*, we have three paragraphs of which Hee-jin Kim states that they "express the gist of the entire *Genjō-kōan* fascicle and, for that matter, of the whole Shōbōgenzō."[4] We need to take a prolonged look at these paragraphs to see what the implications of that statement are.

When all dharmas are the Buddha-dharma, there is illusion and enlightenment, contemplation and action, birth and Death, buddhas and sentient beings.

When myriad dharmas are of the nonself, there is no illusion or enlightenment, no buddhas or sentient beings, no arising or perishing.

Because the Buddha-way intrinsically leaps out of plenitude and dearth, there is arising and perishing, illusion and enlightenment, sentient beings and buddhas. Still do flowers fall to our pity and weeds grow to our displeasure.[5]

The first paragraph states the duality and differentiation of illusion and enlightenment, meditation or contemplation and action in the world, birth and death, buddhas (enlightenment), and sentient beings (illusion). Differentiation is the case when dharmas are of the Buddha-dharma. This may be cautiously compared to a "thesis," a positive statement.

The second paragraph negates the first in that it asserts the nonduality and nondifferentiation of illusion (sentient beings) and enlightenment (buddhas) and arising and perishing. Now, nonduality is the case when dharmas are of the nonself. This can be compared to a negation of the thesis, to an antithesis. The first paragraph asserts "is"; the second paragraph asserts "is not." But the second paragraph is not the simple negation of the first. Illusion (sentient beings) and enlightenment (buddhas) are common to both paragraphs; contemplation and action are absent from the second paragraph and are thus never explicitly negated. The first paragraph speaks of birth and death, whereas the second negates, not precisely birth and death, but arising and perishing. Whereas the affinities between birth and arising and between death and perishing are obvious, its remains questionable whether they can simply be "equated." All of this is mentioned in order to point out that the second paragraph is not simply a global negation of the first.

The third paragraph is no "synthesis" of the first two. The Buddha-way "leaps out" of plentitude (form, differentiation, and duality, "is" first paragraph) and dearth (emptiness, nonduality, "is not," second paragraph). What does Dōgen mean by "leaping out?" Instead of synthesizing the first two paragraphs, the third dynamically transcends them (neither "is" nor "is not"). Yet the final sentence of that paragraph indicates that form, duality, and emptiness (nonduality) are still present, are included as well (both "is" and "is not"). Flowers wither and die while weeds flourish. Things do not conform to what we want; they are not just the way we would like them to be. They simply are as they are (suchness).

It should finally be noted that birth and death and contemplation and action are never specifically negated as such. Thus, there is subtle differentiation within Dōgen's "dialectic."

We shall consider the next two paragraphs of *Genjō-kōan*, saving the remaining paragraphs for a later discussion with a somewhat broader focus.

> To exert and verify myriad dharmas by carrying forth the self is illusion; to exert and verify the self while myriad dharmas come forth is enlightenment. Those who apply illusion to great enlightenment are buddhas; those who have great illusion amid enlightenment are sentient beings. Furthermore, there are persons who attain enlightenment upon enlightenment; there are persons who have more illusion within illusion.[6]

The focus of this paragraph is clearly illusion and enlightenment. Illusion consists in carrying forth the self, in asserting the self and attempting to force exertion and verification of myriad dharmas or things. This is deluded activity, the very opposite of what the Taoists called "*wu wei*," noninterference or letting be (Meister Eckhart's *Gelassenheit*), which is nothing passive. What should come forth is not the self, but the myriad dharmas. What should be exerted and verified are not the dharmas, but the self. The self is to be *exerted*, not *asserted*.

Activity of the Self

We need to pause in our interpretation of the beginning of *Genjō-kōan* and consider briefly the three related terms "total exertion" (*gūjin*), "activity-unremitting," "ceaseless practice" (*gyōji*), and "total dynamism" (*zenki*). Kim broaches the extremely subtle differentiation between total exertion (*gūjin*) and total life force/dynamism (*zenki*) as follows:

> Thus, the principles of the total exertion and the total function or dynamism are two aspects of the one and same reality of subjectivity in Dōgen's metaphysical realism. Loosely speaking, the former addresses itself primarily to the self, whereas the latter (the total dynamism) speaks to the world. Both refer to the undefiled freedom and liberation of the self and the world as the self-expression of Buddha-nature.[7]

The expression "two aspects of one and the same reality of subjectivity," I believe, must be taken to mean that, whether the emphasis is on self or on world, the "place" where Buddha-nature expresses itself is ultimately localized in the self which is inseparable from world. Otherwise we are back in the dualism of subject and object, which cannot be Kim's intention.

If we provisionally accept for now this "loose statement" that exertion refers more to self and dynamism more to world, where does that leave our third term, activity-unremitting? Again referring to Kim, activity-unremitting is "the universal dynamics inherent in all reality."[8] Thus, activity-unremitting would seem to be the most comprehensive of the three terms. Certainly the fascicle on activity-unremitting constitutes one of the longer and more substantial of the Shōbōgenzō, whereas the fascicle on total dynamism is quite short and there is no separate fascicle on total exertion at all.

Having made this general statement, we want to briefly examine each of the three terms. The following cursory discussion can hardly exhaust the matter.

Total exertion (gūjin)

Although no separate fascicle is devoted to it, total exertion certainly pervades the whole of Shōbōgenzō. Exertion often seems to be roughly equivalent to self-obstruction and is inseparable from a dharma-situation (*jūhōi*). Exertion and a continuous flowing on of temporal activity preclude each other. In other words, in order for a thing to totally exert itself or to obstruct itself, it must achieve a certain *stasis*, a dwelling where it abides in its dharma-situation. For example, the act of dropping off the body-mind (*Shinjin datsuraku*) cannot take place in any kind of horizontal transition, but "dropping" definitely implies a vertical dimension where body-mind can actually be let fall. As long as I drag body-mind along with me, which is what I habitually do, body-mind cannot drop off.

Since this is for the moment to be a brief excursion into our three terms, we can say for now that what is perhaps most distinctive about exertion is its inseparability from a dharma-situation and its ultimate identity with self-obstruction and penetration, both terms that we have not yet had the opportunity to discuss.

In a brief discussion Francis Cook gives an interesting interpretation of *gūjin* in his book *How to Raise an Ox*.

> Looked at from the angle of the person who experiences the situation, it means that one identifies one hundred percent with the circumstance. Looked at from the standpoint of the situation itself, the situation is totally manifested or exerted without obstruction or contamination.[9]

The person experiencing a situation totally becomes it. He is not thinking *about* it; he *is* it. When he does this, the situation is completely revealed and manifested. This much is reasonably clear. What does it mean to say that a situation is totally exerted? Normally we associate exertion primarily with human beings, in a secondary sense with some animals. A student exerts himself cramming for an exam. A football player exerts himself running for the touchdown. A husky might exert himself pulling a dogsled with a heavy load. We would not ordinarily speak of a flower exerting itself. How can a situation which is supposedly something "inert and lifeless" or "nonliving" exert itself? We need a viable example here. Suppose a person sensitive to the beauty of nature takes a walk in the forest. Dōgen could have said that the person responding with all of his sensibilities is exerting himself. Here exerting himself does not mean straining or forcing himself, but rather opening himself up. Responding is never anything passive, but can even be quite strenuous. What about the forest? The response of the person allows the forest to become manifest. This becoming manifest does not mean simply putting in an appearance in some static manner, but entails a dynamic presencing. The forest manifests itself actively, that is, it exerts itself and presences fully.

This situation is an "example" of "the whole being of emptiness leaping out of itself" (*konshinchoshutsu*).[10] The term "example," however, is, strictly speaking, inappropriate here since we are not talking about a particular situation exemplifying some universal. The particular situation *is* the whole. Totality presences in it with nothing left out.

We did not discuss the phrase "without obstruction or contamination." A discussion of "obstruction" will be saved for a later context. "No contamination" simply means that nothing extraneous leaks into the total situation.

Total Dynamism (zenki)

What seems to stand out most about total dynamism is that it is primarily related to birth and death, which certainly constitute, after all, an important part of the most basic structure of existence. Like the dropping-off of the body-mind, birth and death for

Dōgen are in no way transitions, birth being ordinarily conceived as a transition into life and death as a transition and passage out of it. Birth and death never obstruct each other, nor does one birth obstruct any other birth or one death any other death.

> This dynamic working (*kikan*) makes birth and death what they truly are. . . . The present moment's birth exists in this dynamic working; dynamic working exists in the present moment's birth. Birth is neither a coming nor a going; birth is neither a manifestation nor a completion. Nonetheless, birth is the presence of total dynamism, death is the presence of total dynamism. (Kim, 242)

Although the present moment's birth exists in this dynamic working and dynamic working exists in the present moment's birth, Dōgen unambiguously asserts the priority of dynamic working over birth and death (it makes them what they truly are). He makes a similar statement in the *Gyōji* fascicle:

> We should study that we see birth-and-death in the en-actment of the Way; we do not enact the Way in birth-and-death. . . . (195)

> Conditioned arising is activity-unremitting, because activity-unremitting is not caused by conditioned arising. (193)

Whatever else Dōgen intended with these kinds of statements, he is attempting to eliminate "humans' petty views" (245). One of the most tenacious of these views is that of a stretch of time between birth and death in which things occur. Birth and death thus constitute a static, extended framework within which various things can happen. A careful study of the *uji*-fascicle should help to undermine our traditional, hopelessly narrow views. There is no temporal duration and, consequently, no stretch of time in which things occur, no transition from one thing or period to another. Spring is spring and summer is summer; spring does not become summer. Birth is birth and death is death; birth does not become death.

However, we do not wish to become too involved with the question of time at this point. That subject pervades everything that Dōgen wrote, and we shall return to it after investigating the activity of the self as far as we can.

Oddly enough, the meaning of moon (*tsuki*) in the *tsuki*-fascicle is nearly identical to total dynamism (*zenki*). Our metaphysically conditioned minds immediately want to construe "moon" as a symbol, a metaphor for total dynamism, or at least an example of it. But this will not do. In Kim's words,

> Since its first ideographic component *tsu* or *to* means "all," "total," etc., and the second component *ki* is as in *zenki* ("total dynamism"), we may well conjecture that Dōgen is here alluding to *zenki* by way of the moon metaphor. . . . Dōgen here relates *nyo* ("like") to *ze* ("this"), evoking the familiar Zen association *nyoze* ("like this," "thusness"). He goes on to draw the implication that "like this" signifies not mere resemblance but the nondual identity of symbol and symbolized. He thus rejects any dualistic notion of metaphor or simile (*hiyu*), whereby an image points to, represents, or approximates something other than itself. Rather, for Dōgen, the symbol itself *is* the very *presence* of total dynamism, i.e., it *presents*. (250–51)

Total dynamism is not some kind of universal that is exemplified or symbolized by the moon. Such a universal does not exist for Dōgen. Rather, moon together with clouds scudding by or moon and the myriad forms it illuminates constitute a dharma-situation that utterly lacks a causal structure. For Dōgen, it is not the case that clouds scudding by cause us to believe that the moon is moving. There is no hierarchy here or, for that matter, anywhere else in Dōgen's thought. Hierarchy is just another remnant of metaphysical thinking, another form of an *arche* or principle.

As in the fascicle on total dynamism, in the moon-fascicle Dōgen takes up the dharma-situation of a boat in water. It is significant that both fascicles present this situation; this attests to their cohesion. The situation of the boat in water explicitly includes the human being sailing the boat, whereas the situation of moon and scudding clouds does so less explicitly. Without explanation "moon" suddenly becomes "mind-moon." Dōgen's emphasis is always predominantly cosmological; it is never anthropocentric. When speaking of human beings, he is mostly concerned with getting his listeners to distance themselves from the narrow-minded and petty views of humans, and even of gods.

The common theme of the three activities focused on here: total exertion, total dynamism, and activity-unremitting, is the kind of "movement" involved. Words like "activity," "dynamism," and "exertion" indicate that something is "going on." "Dynamism" is too abstract to provide a concrete sense of what Dōgen is trying to convey. We can, however, bear the Greek sense of *dynamis* in mind if we extract it from the Aristotelian schema of *dynamis-energeia*, potentiality-actuality. Potentiality or potency in Dōgen is not geared to actualizing itself. Potency *is* actual. Everything is right now (*nikon*), not off in the future "somewhere."

The Tathagata's statement that "The moon moves when clouds scud, and the shore passes when a boat sails" is such that the "clouds scudding" is the "moon's moving," and the "boat's sailing" is the "shore's passing." Cloud and moon walk and move together, at the same time, on the same path, and have nothing to do with beginning or end, before or after; boat and shore walk and move together, at the same time, on the same path, and have noth-

ing to do with starting or stopping, flowing or returning."(248–49)

We must face and grapple with the question of what potency
is if it is not geared to actualization as its "not yet." What kind of
"movement" is involved in potency? We ordinarily think of
movement as something that starts and stops, that begins and
ends. We ordinarily think that all movement goes somewhere,
makes a transition. This kind of movement presupposes a continuity and a substratum that Dōgen absolutely rejects. Thus, he
can state that "'Clouds' scudding is not concerned with east,
west, south or north" (249). We are not talking about any kind of
direction or local motion in general. Dōgen presents another situation where our customary way of thinking movement simply
cannot apply. That situation is the mountain's walking. Anyone
knows that a mountain is not about to pick itself up and trudge
in some direction. The mountain's "walking" must be of a different sort.

Those who doubt the mountain's walking do not yet
know their own walking. It is not that they do not walk
but that they do not know or understand their own
walking. (296)

Because we do not understand our own "walking," we cannot conceive of what it means to say that a mountain walks. And
yet we still do walk even though we do not understand this.
Thus, we are speaking of some sort of "automatic" or at least non-
conscious or non-deliberate activity here. Dōgen also uses the
term "working" to describe what the mountain does. This seems
somewhat less paradoxical, also less forceful. If for "walking"
and "working" we try to substitute "presencing," this might help
to facilitate our understanding. A mountain has a definite presence, as does a person without making a conscious effort. There is
a distinct kind of "power" in this presencing that links it to the

dynamis or potency we were trying to bring out. We shall return to this absolutely central issue later.

Activity-unremitting (*gyōji*)

Like *uji*, being-time, which takes place constantly regardless of the enlightened or unenlightened state of things and persons, total dynamism and activity-unremitting would appear to be constantly at work, whereas total exertion seems at times to be less "automatic," seems to require some kind of concerted "effort." Thus, whereas the word "total" in total dynamism would appear to refer to the "universality" of that dynamism, "total" in total exertion appears more to indicate the entirety and wholeness of a single dharma. This is most evident in the phrase *"ippogūjin*," the total exertion of a single thing, a favorite expression of Dōgen's.

This is not to say that total exertion is a matter of someone's "will" or forcible doing; none of these three terms has anything to do with that. Rather, exertion has to do with *enactment*. Enactment is the taking place (*kyōryaku*) or, if you like, the embodiment or bodying of absolute emptiness. Any ordinary everyday position or situation of time (*uji*) takes its place as a dharma-situation through the total exertion enacting absolute emptiness (*sūnyatā*).

To return to activity-unremitting, the working of *gyōji* is the nonsubstantial "foundation" for everything: self, other, the cosmos. Yet we are not merely passive "products" and puppets of this activity; our own working works along with it. "Because of our activity-unremitting the ring of the Way is possessed of its power" (192).

If, as we have asserted, activity-unremitting is constantly active, whether we are aware of it or not, then what is its relationship to the now, to the present moment? A striking parallel can be found here between activity-unremitting and Buddha-nature in their temporal constitution.

Thus ("all existence") is not a being originally existent because it fills the past and present; not a being arising for the first time because it does not receive a single particle of dust; not a being in isolation because it appropriates all; not a being existing without a beginning because "the What presents itself as it is," not a being existing with a beginning because "One's everyday mind is the Way." (68)

All existence cannot be equated with or restricted to an origin; it has not always been there because it is open-ended without any final limit. All existence does not now originate for the first time because it already contains all that can be. All existence does not exist in isolation because it is interdependent. All existence is not without a beginning because it simply is as it is (suchness). All existence does not have a beginning since everyday mind, which is the Way, has always existed.

The present of activity-unremitting is not an original being abiding primordially in one's self nor is the present of activity-unremitting something going from or coming to, entering or leaving, one's self. What we speak of as the present does not exist prior to activity-unremitting; it is called the present in which activity-unremitting realizes itself. (193–94)

The present of activity-unremitting is not something that we inherently possess; nor is it something extraneous to us that enters the scene at some appropriate moment. It does not exist prior to activity-unremitting; it cannot be separated and isolated by itself. This presents something of a dilemma to our minds accustomed to Aristotelian logic. We would like to seize upon one of two alternatives: either something is innate in us, always with us, or we acquire it at some point as it happens to us. But the present of activity-unremitting cannot be bifurcated into a present moment and an activity-unremitting, both tenuously held together at times by a nebulous "self." There is no present moment that lacks activity-unremitting, whether we are aware of that activity or not.

The Self as Illusion and Enlightenment

We now return to the last two sentences of our passage from *Genjō-kōan*.

> Those who apply illusion to great enlightenment are buddhas; those who have great illusion amid enlightenment are sentient beings. Furthermore, there are persons who attain enlightenment upon enlightenment; there are persons who have more illusion within illusion. (51)

The phrase "those who apply illusion to great enlightenment" refers to buddhas who know how to use illusion and make it work for great enlightenment. For Dōgen, illusion is not nothing and is not useless; it has its own status in reality.

> Thus, while encountering this discourse on dreams in dreams, those who try to eschew the Buddha-way think that some nonexistent phantasms are unreasonably believed to exist and that illusions are piled up on top of illusions. This is not true. Even though delusions are multiplied in the midst of delusions, you should certainly ponder upon the path of absolute freedom (*tshūshī no ro*) in which absolute freedom is apprehended as the very consummation of delusions (*madoi no ue no madoi*).[11]

It is not the case that there are two mutually exclusive states: enlightenment and illusion. Enlightenment and illusion cannot be separated. Dōgen reinterpreted the statement in the Nirvana Sutra: "all beings have the Buddha-nature" to mean: "all beings are the Buddha-nature." We are all fundamentally enlightened. This was Dōgen's own "personal" kōan. If we possess the Buddha-nature already, what need is there for practice? To give a somewhat limping analogy, the Buddha-nature might be compared to a great talent or gift. Suppose that Mozart had decided to become a banker and had never received any musical training or even exposure to music. Mozart undeniably had one of the greatest of musical gifts, and yet it is conceivable that he might never have had the opportunity to develop that gift. Without practice and realization the gift remains dormant. We would be left with a tragic waste.

Now, what does it mean to have great illusion amid enlightenment? It goes without saying that the reflections offered in this study at best point out one of many possible interpretations of Dōgen's rich text which can never be exhausted by some non-indigenous contemporary effort.

To have great illusion amid enlightenment could mean that someone is deluded about their supposed enlightenment, that someone is convinced that he is enlightened, whereas, in fact, he is not. Probably Zen masters' experience abounds with such examples. The expressions "Zen sickness," "the stink of Zen" confirm the fact that there has been an ample supply of such cases. The most poisonous kind of ego-pride is spiritual pride.

This might also be applicable to the last statement in our passage: There are persons who have more illusion within illusion. To have more illusion within illusion might well mean that a person has no idea that he is deluded. A person who realizes that he is deluded is no longer completely within the realm of illusion. As Socrates remarked, he knew that he knew nothing. In part this remark was ironical. Nobody ever got the best of Socrates in an argument or a discussion. But on a more profound level, Socrates meant this seriously. After all, when it comes to ultimate questions none of us ordinary mortals knows anything.

Finally, we come to the last remaining statement: there are persons who attain enlightenment upon enlightenment. The basic sense of this would appear to be that of no attachment to enlightenment, ultimate freedom from the idea of something labeled "enlightenment."

Attaining enlightenment beyond enlightenment is also characterized as going beyond the Buddha. In the fascicle bearing that title (*Bukkōjōji*) Dōgen writes:

> This one who goes beyond the Buddha is the "non-Buddha." When you are asked what the non-Buddha is like, just consider: We do not call him/her the non-Buddha because s/he exists before the Buddha, nor do we call him/her the non-Buddha because s/he exists after the Buddha; nor is s/he the non-Buddha because s/he outreaches the Buddha. S/he is the non-Buddha only because s/he goes beyond the Buddha. This non-Buddha is known as such because s/he drops off the Buddha's countenance and because s/he drops off the Buddha's body-mind.[12]

"Going beyond" is not to be considered as any kind of transcendence in the traditional sense. The whole import of Dōgen's key term "dropping off" is diametrically opposed to "climbing over" (*trans-cendere*) and refreshingly obviates meta-physics, trans-meta-physics, meta-meta-meta-physics and the whole business of "meta" of which it is to be fervently hoped we have truly had our philosophical fill. Kim's footnote is helpful here.

> The process of going beyond the Buddha is not a matter of temporal sequence any more than it is one of spatial juxtaposition. The "beyond" defies any static spatial or temporal analogies. This view is quite consistent with Dōgen's notion of temporal passage (*kyōryaku*). Elsewhere in this fascicle he writes: "This process of going beyond the Buddha is to reach the Buddha while advancing to meet the Buddha anew.[13]

Again, we postpone discussion of temporal passage (*kyōryaku*) until a later point when we shall take up the question of being-time (*uji*) pervading all of Dōgen's writings.

> When you have unsurpassed wisdom, you are called buddha. When a buddha has unsurpassed wisdom, it is called unsurpassed wisdom. Not to know what it is like on this path is foolish. What it is like is to be unstained. To be unstained does not mean that you try forcefully to exclude intention or discrimination, or that you establish a state of nonintention. Being unstained cannot be intended or discriminated at all.
>
> Being unstained is like meeting a person and not considering what he looks like. Also it is like not wishing for more color or brightness when viewing flowers or the moon.[14]

Being unstained is not something that can be consciously willed or brought about; any intention simply precludes it. Dōgen says that being unstained is like meeting a person and not considering what he looks like. Mostly when we meet someone, particularly for the first time, but also subsequently in a different way, we "take stock" and "keep score." What strikes us are categories and above all numbers: how old the person is, whether thin or fat, what color hair and eyes, plus ensuing informational data such as profession or job, how much his or her salary is, what kind of house he or she lives in, married or single, children *ad infinitum malum*. We should just meet a person as he is in his suchness without considering all the categories and numbers which have little or nothing to do with who that "person" is. After all, person comes from *personare*, to sound through, whence comes the idea of *persona* or mask. We want to meet "what sounds through."

Similarly, we should not wish for more color in the flowers or more brightness in the moon, This "more" is our idealized category, and misses the flowers and the moon in their suchness, their as-it-is-ness. Overpainting the landscape ruins the painting. Or one can perhaps see this as-it-is-ness in a small child before it has become self-conscious. It just *is*, and that is its utter charm.

> Spring has the tone of spring, and autumn has the tone of autumn; there is no escaping it. So when you want spring or autumn to be different from what it is, notice that it can only be as it is. Or when you want to keep spring or autumn as it is, reflect that it has no unchanging nature.[15]

Dōgen chooses the most volatile and transitional seasons of the year, the seasons where we are most apt to notice nature. Winter and summer seem to be more stable, even somewhat static. But if I want autumn to be spring and not autumn, I am simply deluding myself and lose the reality of what is. And if I want to hang onto spring, keep it and not let it give way to summer, I have failed to realize that nothing can have an unchanging nature. Impermanence *is* Buddha-nature.

> That which is accumulated is without self, and no mental activity has self. The reason is not that one of the four great elements or the five *skandhas* can be understood as self or identified as self. Therefore, the form of the flowers or the moon in your mind should not be understood as being self, even though you think it is self. Still, when you clarify that there is nothing to be disliked or longed for, then the original face is revealed by your practice of the Way.[16]

Here Dōgen eliminates both the physical and mental components (the four great elements and the five skandhas—that which is accumulated) and also specific mental activity such as representing images of flowers or the moon as envisioned by something like the self. This is a more detailed and explicit way of describing the dropping off of body and mind. Whereas Plato had singled out the immortal soul as what is real, as what is the self, and had denigrated the body to being "the prison of the soul" (*Phaedo* 81 e), Dōgen wants to free one from *both* body and mind. What we think of as our mind, the mental activity and representation going on more or less automatically in our heads is not what we truly are, is not the self. It, too, must be dropped off. Take, for example, James Joyce's *Ulysses.* This enormous book describes what went on in one man's head during a period of twenty-four hours. Can we therefore say that this is what the man is?

> Also learn that the entire universe is the dharma body of the self. To seek to know the self is invariably the wish of living beings. However, those who see the true self are rare. Only buddhas know the true self.
>
> People outside the way regard what is not the self as the self. But what buddhas call the self is the entire universe. Therefore, there is never an entire universe that is not the self, with or without our knowing it. On this matter defer to the words of the ancient buddhas.[17]

Dōgen is keenly aware that he is writing for students of the Way, not for enlightened buddhas. He is concerned with what those students understand and do not understand, and admonishes them again and again:

> Yet the ancient buddha's word cannot be mistaken. Even if you do not understand it, you should not ignore it. So, be determined to understand it. Since this word is already expounded, you should listen to it. Listen until you understand.[18]

Any performing musician knows that he has to practice until he "gets it right." How many students of philosophy and religion realize that they ought to do the same?

The self is the entire universe. Is this not an outlandish, far-fetched and trumped-up statement? Not at all. We all begin by thinking that this particular being that I myself am is the self. But the true self is formless. Thus, *it cannot be a being*. This is extremely difficult to fathom because all we know and talk about are specific beings. This was Martin Heidegger's gargantuan difficulty with regard to the question of being. He knew that being can never be a being (ontological difference), he also brought being very close to nothingness (the veil of being) on various occasions, but he was never able to follow the radicality of the Buddhist approach—to present a "positive" dimension of nothingness, admittedly a very difficult thing to do.

What is not the self is this particular being that I think I am. Even the Upanishads say that the Self is *neti, neti*, not this particular being, not that particular being, not a being at all. And, of course, the Buddha himself taught that all beings have no self (*anatman*). But this does not mean that the self is nothing, which would commit the sin of nihilism, just as the opposing statement that the self is a real, permanent being commits the sin of permanence or eternalism.

After explaining that fish always know one another's heart, unlike people who do not know one another's heart, and stating that a bird can see traces of hundreds and thousands of small birds whereas beasts have no conception of what traces in the sky are, Dōgen goes on:

> Buddhas are like this. You may wonder how many lifetimes buddhas have been practicing. Buddhas large and small, although they are countless, all know their own traces. You never know a buddha's trace when you are not a buddha.
>
> You may wonder why you do not know. The reason is that, while buddhas see these traces with a buddha's eye, those who are not buddhas do not have a buddha's eye, and just notice the buddha's attributes.

All who do not know should search out the trace of a buddha's path. If you find footprints, you should investigate whether they are the buddha's. On being investigated, the buddha's trace is known; and whether it is long or short, shallow or deep, is also known. To illuminate your trace is accomplished by studying the buddha's trace. Accomplishing this is buddha-dharma.[19]

In contrast to the usual meaning of "trace" as residue, something left over or behind, a kind of defilement, to know the Buddha's trace is to know his path, to know where he has gone. After all, Dōgen's examples of fish knowing where fish are going and birds knowing one another's traces do not constitute "traces" that any of us can discern.

We cannot see the Buddha's traces because we see the Buddha from the outside. All we see are attributes, not traces. This should remind us of the passage previously discussed about meeting a person and not considering what he looks like. This is to be unstained.

"Traces" may also remind us of the Oxherding pictures in which a boy first catches sight of the footprints of the ox and thus begins his quest for the true self. Before he saw the footprints he might well have not known that there was anything to look for.

The Self as Buddha-nature

Concentrating mainly on the Buddha-nature fascicle with occasional passages from elsewhere, we now want to explore to a certain extent what Dōgen says about the self as Buddha-nature. Probably the most obvious thing about Buddha-nature is the fact that it does not coincide with the individual ego-self. But the traditional Western and Hindu alternative, that is, to say that the Buddha-nature is a Universal Self will not do either. The matter is far more subtle and more difficult.

They [many students] think vainly that the Buddha-
nature's enlightenment and awakening is the same as the
conscious mind which is only the movement of wind and
fire. But who has said that there is in the Buddha-nature
enlightenment and awakening! Although enlightened
ones and awakened ones are buddhas, still the Buddha-
nature is neither enlightenment nor awakening in the ordinary sense.[20]

If the student attempts to look into his mind, and this is what
he is instructed to do if he is not to search for the Buddha-nature
outside of himself, what he encounters is the ordinary mind's re-
actions to what is going on around him. In other words, in spite of
his attempt to "turn within," he is still "outside." Actually, the
very fact that he is representing an "outside" and an "inside" dualistically, shows that he is getting nowhere. He is trying to enter
what Heidegger called "the cabinet of consciousness." However,
as Heidegger showed throughout *Being and Time,* we are always
already "out there" (in the world). This is the meaning of ek-sis-
tence and ek-stasis. The cabinet of consciousness is a Cartesian
construct.

It has often happened that . . . those who have been
teachers to men and devas . . . have, many of them,
thought that the wind and fire movement of man's conscious mind is the Buddha-nature's enlightenment. It is to
be pitied, that such a blunder occurred because they have
not paid sufficient heed to the study of the Way.
Advanced students and beginners in the Buddha
Way must not make this mistake now. Even though you
may study enlightenment, enlightenment is not the wind
and fire movement of the conscious mind. Even though
you study movement, it is not what you think it is. If you
can understand movement in its truth, then you can also
understand true enlightenment and awakening.[21]

A kind of "everyday" kōan is the question: Who am I? In Zen this is often expressed as: Where do you come from? This, of course, is not a question about geography; it is a question about the self. Even in contemporary slang when someone says: I know where you are coming from, this means basically that he knows "where" and who the person *is*.

> When the Sixth Chinese Patriarch Ta-chien Ch'an-shih of Ts'ao-hsi shan first went to practice under the Fifth Patriarch of Huang-mei shan, he was asked, "Where do you come from?" He answered, "I am a man of Ling-nan." The Fifth Patriarch said, "What have you come for?" "I've come to become a Buddha," he replied. The Fifth Patriarch said, "People of Ling-nan have no Buddha-nature. How could you attain Buddhahood?"[22]

Dōgen interprets this to mean, not that people from Ling-nan have no Buddha-nature, but that the Sixth Patriarch is no-Buddha-nature. This is similar to his interpretation of the Nirvana Sutra's saying, "All sentient beings without exception have the Buddha-nature," to mean all beings or whole being is the Buddha-nature. Buddha-nature is nothing that we possess already or that we acquire through practice; the Buddha-nature is manifested at the very moment of attainment. The categories of our logical, conceptual thinking compel us to ask: either we always possess it or else we first acquire it through attainment. Many of the kōans, especially the one about polishing a tile, stress the impossibility of acquiring or becoming the Buddha-nature. It just flashes up at the moment of our seeing. Seeing and flashing up are one sudden, instantaneous "event." We shall return to this crucial point in a discussion of form and emptiness. Emptiness is not an entity; it is manifest only in form. Similarly, the Buddha-nature is no entity whatsoever; it manifests itself only in seeing.

Another way of asking who someone is or where he comes from is to ask his name.

Then, when he [the Fifth patriarch] was seven years old, while on the way to Huang-mei mountain, he met the Fourth Patriarch Ta-i, who saw that although he was still a child, his physiognomy was excellent and unusual, different from that of ordinary children. The patriarch asked him, "What is your name?" The boy replied, "There is a name, but it is not an ordinary name." The master said, "What name is it?" "It is Buddha-nature," said the boy. The patriarch said, "You have no Buddha-nature." The boy replied, "You say no (Buddha-nature) because Buddha-nature is emptiness."[23]

When asked for his name, the boy does not reply that he *has* a name, but states that *there is* a name, that is, Buddha-nature. The master flatly retorts that the boy has no Buddha-nature. But the boy, instead of being rebuked or defeated by that remark, replies that he "has" no-Buddha-nature because Buddha-nature is emptiness. Here again "no-Buddha-nature" must be understood to lie beyond the opposition of Buddha-nature versus no-Buddha nature.

Dōgen continues:

You must without fail devote yourself to the truth of "no-Buddha-nature," never remitting your efforts. No-Buddha-nature has to be traced perplexingly, yet it does have a touchstone: "What." It has a time: "You." There is entering into its dynamic functioning: "Affirmation." . . .

The Fifth Patriarch said, "You say no (Buddha-nature) because Buddha-nature is emptiness." This clearly and distinctly articulates the truth: that is, emptiness is not, "no." But in uttering "Buddhanature-emptiness," one says "no." One does not say "half a pound" or "eight ounces." One does not say emptiness, because it is emptiness. One does not say no because it is no. One says no because it is Buddhanature-emptiness.

Thus, each piece of no is a touchstone to articulate
emptiness; emptiness is the power articulating no.[24]

Dōgen is asking how we can understand no-Buddha-nature.
The basic structure here is already familiar to us: we must trace
the no-Buddha-nature that is beyond the opposition of Buddha-
nature and no Buddha-nature. That can be expressed as Buddhanature-emptiness. This Buddhanature-emptiness is not just some
kind of empty space or gaping abyss. It articulates itself. It has a
touchstone, that is, What. What could be any specific occasion.
But Buddhanature-emptiness can never be equated with any specific What. Buddhanature-emptiness has a time, that is, you, any
human being who is open to it. Finally, we can enter into the dynamic functioning of Buddhanature-emptiness. We participate in
or, more exactly, we *are* that dynamic functioning. In that we are
it, we affirm it and this affirmation, again, is beyond the duality of
affirmation and negation.

Emptiness is not "no"; it cannot be equated with any specific
thing or with that thing's negation. But when we come to express
it, we say "no." This is preferable to saying something particular
such as half a pound or eight ounces. Neither emptiness nor no
can be expressed directly in ordinary language. Thus, we do not
say no, because it is no. We do not say emptiness, because it is
emptiness. Although emptiness is not no, each piece of no is a
touchstone to articulate emptiness. Emptiness is the power articulating no.

The "power" of emptiness must not be understood as some
kind of potentiality or *dynamis* in the Aristotelian sense of part of
the structure of *dynamis-energeia* or an entelechy. There is no continuous process involved here. Strictly speaking, emptiness does
not *become* form. No-thing cannot become some-thing in any ordinary sense.

In an article entitled "The Characteristics of Oriental Nothingness," Shin' ichi Hisamatsu, who was the one to centrally use
the expression "Formless Self," states that the characterization of

empty space, while applicable, is not of itself sufficient to express oriental nothingness. Oriental nothingness is not only alive, which empty space is not, but also and above all *aware*. It has nothing to do with what we normally take to be the subject, but is fundamentally a *seeing*.

> Thus, the True Nature is always free, and further, because "seeing into one's True Nature," not being any-thing, is every-thing, and being every-thing, is not any-thing. It is in this sense that the true meaning of "absolute negation is in itself absolute affirmation and absolute affirmation is in itself absolute negation" is to be understood.[25]

Hisamatsu also repeatedly stresses the fact that it is of the utmost importance to negate the usual state of human being, all vestiges of the anthropocentric idealism prevalent in the modern age and especially psychologism that will never escape anthropocentricism, but will flatly reduce anything holy or divine to a wish-fantasy or a pathological state of consciousness.

> Above I mentioned Zen as being a religion of "man simply being Buddha" which negates the "holy" and transcendent and does not search for the Buddha separated from or external to man's self. In speaking these words, however, it is not with the intention of affirming the notion that man in his usual state is Buddha, the view of anthropocentric idealism prevalent in the modern age, or that the idealized form of man is Buddha. Zen's affirmation of man is not so simplistic. It is the position of Zen rather to negate absolutely the usual state of man. . . . Both of them [Po-chang Huai-hei and Lin-chi] stress strongly the absolute negation of the usual state of man.[26]

The usual state of human being is to be negated, not because humans are sinful or evil, but because they are not awake. They are not even fully and truly alive. Hisamatsu brings out the unique feature of Zen that seeks to overcome the view of the holy or divine as something transcendental and objective completely outside of human being. Thus, Hisamatsu accepts neither the view that the usual state of human being as such is holy nor the view that the holy is something objective and transcendent absolutely separate from human being. The antidote to the first view could be found in Nietzsche's bitterly sarcastic remark: "All men godlike!" Human being in its usual state is not automatically something to be proud of. One has only to take a look at the world as it is today or, for that matter, as it often has been. On the other hand, the idea of the holy as something utterly unattainable is hardly satisfying for the religious seeker here and now.

> On the other hand, Zen takes up neither the deification of man, a position naively assumed in modern times, nor the position of a transcendent God insisted upon by Dialectical Theology. The crucial position of Zen is to affirm the "sacred in man" by retrieving the sacred from the reaches of transcendent views or objective forms and returning it to the folds of human subjectivity.[27]

To return to the more specific issues in Dōgen, the important thing is not whether one speaks of Buddha-nature or no-Buddha-nature. Such discussions get tangled up in the question of existence or nonexistence. A Western counterpart can be found in the disputes about theism versus atheism. They focus solely on existence versus nonexistence and fail to inquire into what is meant by the word "god" or even by the word "existence." They assume that everyone knows who or what a god is.

> He [the Sixth Patriarch] should have set aside the nothingness of "being and nothingness" and asked, What is this Buddha-nature? He should have sought, What sort of

thing is this Buddha-nature? People of today as well, when they hear "Buddha-nature," never question what this Buddha-nature is. They seem to speak only about the meaning of such things as the existence or non-existence of Buddha-nature. That is rash and ill-considered.[28]

One should not get into long disputes about whether Buddha-nature exists or does not exist, but rather ask what kind of thing that could be. How can one argue whether something exists or not when one doesn't know what it is? Is it Mind? It is permanent or impermanent? What does it "do?"

Near the beginning of this chapter we touched upon the question of activity, dynamism, and exertion. We now continue that scrutiny, focusing on the question of impermanence and temporality. "Temporality" indicates how dynamism takes place or comes about. The term "dynamism" by itself is too general to convey a concrete meaning.

Temporality and Impermanence

Even though you study movement, it is not what you think it is. If you can understand movement in its truth, then you can also understand true enlightenment and awakening.[29]

What does movement have to do with awakening? We have already been told that the wind and fire movement of human being's conscious mind is *not* movement in its truth. Movement in its truth is neither motion in the ordinary sense nor stillness in its ordinary sense. It is not a matter of quelling motion and becoming quiescent.

Buddha said, "If you wish to know the Buddha-nature's meaning, you should watch for temporal conditions. If the time arrives, the Buddha-nature will manifest itself." . . .

If you wish to know the Buddha-nature's meaning might be read, "you are directly knowing the Buddha-nature's meaning." You should watch for temporal conditions means "you are directly knowing temporal conditions." If you wish to know the Buddha-nature, you should know that "it is precisely temporal conditions themselves."[30]

Dōgen removes the hypothetical and imperative character from this passage. Instead of saying: if you want this, you should do that, he states: you know it right now. And instead of saying: if you wish to know this, you should watch for temporal conditions, he states: look at the temporal conditions right in front of you or even the temporal conditions that you yourself are. Nothing is postponed to the future. It is not a matter of waiting and watching for something to arrive. It has to be right here now, or else it doesn't "exist" at all. "There has never yet been a time not arrived. There can be no Buddha-nature that is not Buddha-nature manifested right now."[31]

Either Buddha-nature is manifested right now, or "there is" no Buddha-nature. But the latter alternative would not be an alternative for Dōgen; it would just be the deluded pronouncement of an ignorant mind.

The last issue to be discussed in the fascicle on Buddha-nature before turning to the fascicle on being-time is that of permanence-impermanence.

The Sixth Patriarch taught his disciple Hsing-ch'ang, "Impermanence is in itself Buddha-nature. Permanence is, as such, the (dualistic) mind which discriminates all dharmas, good or bad."[32]

The central topic here is impermanence. Here again, however, we must get beyond the traditional dualism of static, persistent being (permanence) and evanescent becoming (impermanence).

To assert permanence is tantamount to asserting eternalism; to assert impermanence in its usual sense is tantamount to asserting nihilism. It is safer to err on the side of impermanence; any assertion of permanence must proceed with extreme caution. Until about the last hundred years, philosophers, at least in the West, have been prone to falling prey to eternalism.

If "permanence" cannot be understood as static persistence and also cannot be understood apart from impermanence, how is it to be conceived? It presences right in the midst of impermanence, yet it itself has nothing to do with traces of coming and going. Permanence is unchanging in the sense that it does not go anywhere or become anything. Its concretization is to be found in *juhōi*, dwelling in a dharma-situation, which embodies the aspect of difference and individuality preventing everything from melting together in a "night in which all cows are black."

> "Do you know," said Hui-neng, "if the Buddha-nature were permanent, what would be the need on top of that to preach about all dharmas good and bad? Even in the elapse of an entire kalpa there would not be a single person who would ever raise the mind in quest of enlightenment. Therefore I preach impermanence, and just that is the way of true permanence preached by the Buddha. On the other hand, if all dharmas were impermanent, then each and every thing would merely have a selfhood and would take part in birth and death, and there would be areas to which true permanence did not reach. Therefore I preach permanence, and it is just the same as the meaning of true impermanence preached by the Buddha."[33]

It is the impermanence and emptiness of Buddha-nature that makes it accessible. If it were permanent and eternal in the sense of a Platonic Form, one could do no more than vainly strive after it. And if everything were hopelessly mired in birth and death with no possibility of a respite, again, Buddha-nature would be inaccessible. Dōgen is on the trail of a sense of permanence and impermanence in which they are ultimately nondual. This sense obviously differs from the ordinary meaning of permanence and impermanence.

Temporality

We turn now to the fascicle on being-time. "We set the self out in array and make that the whole world."[34]

What does it mean to set the self out in array? "Array" seems to imply a positioning of the self in the things of the world. This means that the self is fundamentally "outside" of itself in the world; it is not an encapsulated subject. This self has nothing to do with an isolated subject confronting objects. The eight statements with which the fascicle begins articulate how the self sets itself out in array.

> For the time being, I stand astride the highest mountain peaks.
>> For the time being, I move on the deepest depths of the ocean floor.
>> For the time being, I'm three heads and eight arms.
>> For the time being, I'm eight or sixteen feet.
>> For the time being, I'm a staff or whisk.
>> For the time being, I'm a pillar or lantern.
>> For the time being, I'm Mr. Chang or Mr. Li.
>> For the time being, I'm the great earth and heavens above. (116)

The self sets itself out as various things (staff, whisk, pillar, lantern), as various people (Chang and Li) and as earth and heaven. Hence, this self is not psychological, but cosmological. However, Dōgen then goes on to say that all these "things" are basically so many different times. This completely distances "things" (a neutral term that can include people and the cosmos) from any kind of substantial objects. Time is the most volatile thing imaginable. As Immanuel Kant remarked, it yields no shape. Yet for Dōgen it is not simply volatile, but also contains within itself the possibility of abiding. But abiding has nothing to do with any kind of substance.

Instead of being content with the word "nonsubstantial," we need to ask what that means concretely. If things are time and time is nonsubstantial, this means that things can interpenetrate; they do not obstruct or impede one another. The fact that things can interpenetrate means that they are not necessarily separate and distinct from each other. Dōgen presents the ordinary (deluded) view of time that has its own limited validity.

> He imagines it is like crossing a river and a mountain: while the river and mountain may still exist, I have now passed them by and *I*, at the present time, reside in a fine vermilion palace. To him, the mountain and river and *I* are as far distant as heaven from earth. (119)

This view separates the subject from the various places that he traverses and also separates the present time in which he resides in a fine vermilion palace from the time when he crossed the river and mountain. This common sense view is not totally wrong, but it does not exhaust the matter.

> But the true way of things is not found in this one direction alone. At the time the mountain was being climbed and the river being crossed, I was there in time. The *time* has to *be* in me. Inasmuch as I am there, it cannot be that time passes away. (119)

Wherever the subject is, time, the present, has to be in him. No matter where he is, time is there with him. This present does not exclude, but rather includes past and future. It is not the case that, when I have crossed the river and climbed the mountain and now reside in a fine palace, the river and mountain are separated and far away from me. They are there with me, too. Where I *am*, time does not just pass away.

Dōgen does not explicitly deny the aspect of time that passes away or flies by. But since that aspect of time is the sole one that everybody is aware of, he presents the abiding aspect of time, *juhōi*, dwelling in a dharma-situation, in uncompromisingly paradoxical statements.

Dōgen is dealing with time in its two aspects: the one that everyone is aware of, coming and going, passing away, and the one that he seems to be the first to emphasize in this way, abiding in a dharma-situation. It is true that thinkers in both the West and the East have spoken of an eternal now, but their conception was primarily that of a timeless moment, a moment lifted out of time. Dōgen's abiding in a dharma-situation is unique in that it does not lie outside of time. On the contrary, the present moment (*nikon*) affirms itself while negating past and future and at the same time negates itself while affirming past and future time.

It seems logically comprehensible enough to say that when the present moment affirms itself, it negates past and future; and that when it negates itself, it affirms past and future. But we must ask: What does it mean existentially to say that the present moment affirms or negates itself? The moment is not a human agency. How, then, can it affirm or negate? Obviously not by anything like an act of will. The power of affirmation or negation must be structurally inherent in the moment itself.

Of course, Dōgen does not use abstract terminology like affirm or negate; for negation he uses "swallow down" and for affirmation "spit out." This is not only concrete and pictorial language; it is actually visceral.

> So doesn't the time climbing the mountain or crossing the river swallow down the time of the fine vermilion palace? Doesn't that time spit out this time? (119)

The "dialectic" at stake here takes place between the absolute present (*nikon*) and dwelling in a dharma-situation, and taking place or passage (*kyōryaku*). The ordinary, deluded view of time as merely flying by is, so to speak, a kind of degeneration of passage. When the absolute present affirms itself, a kind of "stasis" or abiding is achieved and dwelling in a dharma-situation results. Past and future are negated, cut off, excluded, yet in some way also included. If they were not in some sense included, the present would be a dimensionless point. What is excluded and negated is the flying by; what is affirmed is dwelling.

Yet time also moves and passes. This is an undeniable fact that everyone and everything experiences and undergoes. In that (one cannot say "when" here) the present negates itself, it opens the gates of the stasis, so to speak, and the past and future embraced in it are freed to move and pass.

> You should not come to understand that time is only flying past. You should not only learn that flying past is the property inherent in time. If time were to give itself to merely flying past, it would have to have gaps. You fail to experience the passage of being-time and hear the utterance of its truth, because you are learning only that time is something that goes past.
>
> The essential point is: every entire being in the entire world is, each time, an (independent) time, even while making a continuous series. (120)

Here Dōgen explicitly states that to think that time is merely flying past is to fail to experience the *passage* of being-time. Thus, passage cannot be equated with flying by. If I experience time as merely flying by, I posit myself as something stationary "watching" time flying past me. I am stationary; time is flying away. The main error here is that I conceive time as something separate from me, as something "in which" I somehow am. This is not Dōgen's understanding at all.

Most people are preoccupied with time's rolling away into the past. They are less aware of the fact that it unfailingly arrives in the present again and again.

> You reckon time only as something that does nothing but pass by, and do not understand it as something not yet arrived. . . . There has never been anyone who, while taking time to be coming and going, has penetrated to see it as a being-time dwelling in its dharma-position. What chance have you then for a time to break through the barrier [to total emancipation?] Even if there were someone who knew that dwelling-position, who would be able truly to give an utterance that preserved what he had thus gained? And even were someone able to give such utterance continually, he still could not help groping to bring his original face into immediate presence. (123)

Dōgen points out two aspects of time unobserved by most people. These two aspects are dwelling in a dharma-position, which has been discussed here to some extent, and not yet arrived. Not yet arrived is obviously the opposite of flying by or passing away, and refers to some kind of "future." What is the aspect of time that is not yet arrived? It could be related to that future of which Plotinus spoke when he said something like: take away the future and human being could not survive. By this Plotinus did not mean the literal truism that if there will be no tomorrow, humans will be physically dead. Rather, like any great mystic, he meant this in an existential sense. Plotinus was not a Christian, so he also did not mean this teleologically or eschatologically. He rather meant something like time in general is something that incessantly comes again and again. What is being emphasized is not the element of the future as something outstanding, but its incessant coming. This is a subtle, but crucial distinction.

> Left entirely to the being-time of the unenlightened, both
> bodhi and nirvana would be being-time which was noth-
> ing more than a mere aspect of going-and-coming. [But]
> no nets or cages long remain—all is the immediate pres-
> encing here and now of being-time. (123)

Again Dōgen emphasizes that seeing only the going-and-
coming aspect of being-time is the unenlightened person's view.
In spite of the unenlightened person's turning even bodhi and
nirvana into a mere aspect of going-and-coming, what really is,
what is real, is the immediate presencing here and now of being-
time. Whatever categories, constructs, and limitations the unenlightened may impose upon being-time, they remain what they
are, that is, delusions fundamentally unable to affect the immediate presencing of being-time.

Passages following again center on the kind of movement involved in the passage of time. Not only is that movement not a
going-and-coming; it does not go anywhere at all.

> In speaking of a "passage": if you imagine the place of
> passage lies somewhere outside, and the dharma of the
> one doing the passage moves toward the east [like the
> spring] through a hundred thousand worlds over a hun-
> dred thousand kalpas of time, that is the result of your
> not giving your singleminded devotion to the sole prac-
> tice of the Buddha Way. (124–25)

The passage in question is an *internal* passage. It does not pass
locally from where it was to where it will be. This already presupposes a conception of time as statically extended, affording a
track or road on which passage occurs.

> Both "reaching" and "not-reaching" are "existence-time."
> Even when the time of "reaching" is not yet over, the time
> of "not-reaching has come. . . . The "reaching" does not

mean coming, nor does the "not-reaching" mean not yet [coming]. Existence-time is like this.[35]

Nothing can possibly be excluded from being-time. If something is not being-time, it simply doesn't exist. Thus, not-reaching as well as reaching is being-time. This passage emphasizes the interpenetration of the modes of time. When reaching or presencing is still going on, not-reaching or coming is arriving in that presencing. Not-reaching expresses the incessant coming of time, its "endlessness." But this not-reaching cannot be equated with a not-yet since it is arriving in presencing. This meaning of the future is better expressed in the French and German, *avenir, Zukunft,* both of which mean literally "to come" or "coming to."

When Dōgen states that a thing impedes itself, he is stressing the self-affirmation and differentiation of the thing. Nothing ever impedes anything else; it only impedes itself. When he speaks of things interpenetrating each other, he is stressing their self-negation and identity with each other. Here there is difference in identity, identity in difference, an idea later developed extensively by the so-called Kyoto school.

We now turn back to the remainder of Genjō-kōan and a somewhat more general discussion of the question of the self.

To learn the Buddha Way is to learn one's own self. To learn one's self is to forget one's self. To forget one's self is to be confirmed by all dharmas. To be confirmed by all dharmas is to effect the casting off of one's own body and mind and the bodies and minds of others as well.

All traces of enlightenment then disappear, and this traceless enlightenment is continued on and on endlessly.[36]

Someone decides to learn about Buddhism and the Buddha Way. In so doing, he discovers the seeker, his own self. Since the Buddha Way is not external to him, this is the inevitable path he follows: He did not set out to study himself, but that is initially what he finds when he seeks to learn about the Buddha Way. The deeper he goes into himself, the more he fails to find anything enduring and substantial. Gradually he "forgets" his self and in this process the things of the world confirm him.

As stated in a previous passage of this fascicle, things have to come to us; we cannot move toward them. Suddenly body and mind drop off, and the person is free. At the same time all others are freed of their bodies and minds as well. When body and mind have thoroughly dropped off, he is not preoccupied with or attached to body-mind or to the dropping off of body-mind, and all traces of enlightenment disappear. He then does not "have" enlightenment, but *is* it. This traceless enlightenment continues on endlessly.

> When a man goes off in a boat and looks back to see the shoreline, he mistakenly thinks the shore is moving. If he keeps his eyes closely on his boat, he realizes it is the boat that is advancing. In like manner, when a person tries to discern and affirm the myriad dharmas with a confused conception of his own body and mind, he mistakenly thinks his own mind and his own nature are permanent. If he makes all his daily deeds intimately his own and returns within himself, the reason that the myriad dharmas are without self will become clear to him.[37]

The man moving along in a boat looks at the shore and mistakenly concludes that it is moving. In reality, of course, it is he who is moving along. His error is due to the fact that he doesn't understand the impermanence and "movement" of his own body and mind. If he will but observe attentively his daily living, he will realize not only that he is by no means permanent, but also that nothing at all is.

We shall consider two further passages from *"Genjō-kōan,"* and then move on to other fascicles. The first concerns the ques-

tion of transition from one state to another which Dōgen, contrary
to all common sense views, flatly denies.

> Once firewood turns to ash, the ash cannot turn back to
> being firewood. Still, one should not take the view that it
> is ashes *afterward* and firewood *before*. He should realize
> that although firewood is at the dharma-stage of fire-
> wood, and that this is possessed of before and after, the
> firewood is beyond before and after. Ashes are in the
> stage of ashes, and possess before and after. Just as fire-
> wood does not revert to firewood once it has turned to
> ashes, man does not return to life after his death. In light
> of this, it being an established teaching in Buddhism not
> to speak of life becoming death, Buddhism speaks of the
> unborn. It being a confirmed Buddhist teaching that
> death does not become life, it speaks of non-extinction.
> Life is a stage of time and death is a stage of time, like, for
> example, winter and spring. We do not suppose that win-
> ter becomes spring, or say that spring becomes summer.[38]

Although firewood "turns to" ash, it does not turn *into* or become ash. This instance of transition is one everyone takes for
granted. Less accessible would be the kind of transition epito-
mized in the kōan about tile-polishing.[39] No one would accept the
idea that polishing a tile would turn it into a mirror. By analogy, it
is not clear to the average person how zazen can transform someone into a Buddha. Dōgen questions every kind of transition, the
kind people take for granted and also the kind that is problematic, and ultimately rejects them all. Firewood is not firewood
before and ashes *afterwards*. Firewood is firewood at the dharma-
situation of firewood and is possessed of before and after which,
so to speak, keep it in that dharma-situation from which it does
not pass. Firewood is "beyond" before and after, a highly enigmatic statement, at least in the sense that it does not pass through
them. Similarly, and far more importantly, life does not become

death nor death become life. (Plato's arguments in the *Phaedo* to
the effect that to the universally accepted fact that what is born,
dies, there belongs the complementary idea that what dies, is re-
born, would not be convincing to Dōgen). Most people who have
watched someone die would surely admit that there is something
utterly incomprehensible involved here. Even the birth of a baby,
which is, after all, not an absolute beginning, always has something astonishing and miraculous about it. On a more mundane
level, who has ever observed *when* winter *became* spring?

> Fish swim the water, and however much they swim, there
> is no end to the water. Birds fly the sky, and however
> much they fly there is no end to the sky. Yet the fish and
> the birds from the first have never left the water and the
> sky. When their need is great there is great activity; when
> their need is small there is small activity. In this way none
> ever fails to exert its every ability, and nowhere does any
> fail to move and turn freely. Yet if a bird leaves the sky it
> quickly dies; if a fish leaves the water it immediately per-
> ishes. We can realize that water means life [for the fish]
> and the sky means life [for the bird]. It must be that the
> bird means life [for the sky], and the fish means life [for
> the water]; that life is the bird and life is the fish. And it
> would be possible to proceed further [in this way]. It is
> similar to this with practice and realization, and with the
> lives of the practicers. Therefore [even] were there a bird
> or fish that wanted to go through the sky or the water
> after studying it thoroughly, it could in sky or water make
> no path, attain no place.[40]

Always distancing himself from any kind of anthropomorphism, Dōgen here considers the perspectives and ways of life of
fish and birds and elsewhere of gods, hungry ghosts, demons. It
is unthinkable that a fish would try to leave the water or a bird
leave the air. Fish and water, bird and air absolutely belong to-

gether. If man can attain the "place" that belongs to him as water belongs to fish and air to birds, his life and actions will then manifest and embody absolute reality.

Nonanthropological Perspectives

In keeping with his complete lack of anthropocentrism, Dōgen investigates not only the perspectives of fish and birds, but also inquires into the "activity" of mountains and waters. He does not relegate mountains and waters to the dubious status of picturesque "landscapes," but considers them thoroughly alive in a manner not identical with human life, yet at the same time nondualistic with it. Again, the categories of identity and difference alone are not sufficiently subtle to encompass what Dōgen wants to convey. Nor is anything gained by attributing to Dōgen some kind of primitive "animism" or "panpsychism." Nothing could be further from the incredible subtlety of his thought.[41]

In the "Mountain and Waters Sutra," Dōgen devotes extensive discussion to "walking." We normally think of walking as motion from one place to another. Since the initial discussion of walking focuses on mountains, this cannot be Dōgen's meaning. What, then, can he mean when he says that mountains always walk? To walk is to go somewhere, but not necessarily in the sense of moving from one place to another. Surely walking is some kind of motion. But I can "go somewhere" without physically moving. This does not mean a fantasy trip of the imagination. In a sense, I am constantly going somewhere, moving, walking because I am alive. We are all constrained by Cartesian categories so that by now the indignant objection is raised: but mountains have no imagination, no mind; they cannot think. But we do not know that. And as Martin Heidegger has pointed out, we do not know what thinking is and as yet we do not think.

As a point of departure, let us try to acknowledge the possibility that mountains are something more and other than dead objects in a landscape. Thus, they "walk."

Mountains do not lack the quality of mountains. Therefore they always abide in ease and always walk. You
should examine in detail this quality of the mountains'
walking. Mountains' walking is just like human walking.
Accordingly, do not doubt mountains' walking even
though it does not look the same as human walking. The
buddha ancestors' words point to walking.[42]

Dōgen is not proffering some idiosyncratic experience of his
own, but appeals here as well to the traditional authority of the
buddha ancestors. In spite of the boldness and often barely intelligible originality of his thought, he never goes against the spirit
of Buddhism and the buddha ancestors. He expands upon and
develops it in the most unforeseeable ways imaginable. Instead of
complaining about unintelligibility and sinking back into our restricted, familiar and worn out ways of representing, thinking,
and experiencing, it should begin to dawn upon us how incredi-
bly limited our experience is. It need not be.

Because green mountains walk, they are permanent. Although they walk more swiftly than the wind, someone in
the mountains does not realize or understand it. "In the
mountains" means the blossoming of the entire world.
People outside the mountains do not realize or understand the mountains' walking. Those without eyes to see
mountains cannot realize, understand, see, or hear this
as it is.

If you doubt mountains' walking, you do not know
your own walking; it is not that you do not walk, but that
you do not know or understand your own walking. Since
you do know your own walking, you should fully know
the green mountains' walking. (98)

Green mountains are said to be "permanent" because their
walking, their activity, is not restricted to a limited span of time.

In a sense, their activity is in principle endless. Someone in the mountains is unable to realize mountains' walking. He is so close to mountains' walking, he is right in the middle of it; thus, he is unable to be aware of it. It is similar to the average person's breathing. He breathes constantly; yet he is unaware of breathing. However, people outside the mountains do not realize or understand the mountains' walking either. Their senses and their minds both fail to perceive even mountains, let along mountains' walking. There are people who "see" mountains, yet do not really see mountains at all. At best they perceive mountains as one object among many. They note that something is objectively there called "mountain." This cannot be called seeing, hearing, realizing, or understanding mountains as they really are.

These people, both those in the mountains and those outside the mountains, doubt mountains' walking. Actually, the idea that mountains walk probably never even occurs to them. In this sense they do not even doubt. However, if we fail to understand mountains' walking, we do not know our own walking. The two cannot be separated. If I cannot understand mountains' walking, then I cannot know my own walking. This does not mean that I do not walk; it just means that I do not understand my walking. But since, after all, I do know something of my own walking, I should study and penetrate the green mountains' walking.

> Green mountains are neither sentient nor insentient. You are neither sentient nor insentient. At this moment, you cannot doubt the green mountains' walking. (98)

This passage simply emphasizes what was already said. Mountains and our selves are not separate. It is not the case that we are sentient whereas mountains are insentient. How could we ever know such a thing? At this moment, right now, we cannot doubt the green mountains' walking.

We might pause to ask an obvious question: why does Dōgen speak specifically of mountains' *walking*? As we stated before, ordinarily no one would *doubt* the green mountains' walking because the very possibility of mountains walking would never occur to him in the first place. However, if someone asserted that mountains walk, *then* he would doubt it. The ordinary person thinks that a mountain "does" nothing. To counteract this attitude, Dōgen describes the mountains' activity in the most specific terms possible: he states that mountains walk. He does not just say that something is going on in the mountains; that is so vaguely expressed that no one would either doubt or believe it. Thus, he states unequivocally: mountains walk. This totally blocks the average person's understanding. He cannot even misunderstand.

Green mountains are neither sentient nor insentient. At this moment, you cannot doubt the green mountains' walking (98).

Again, this passage seeks to undercut the difference between sentient and supposedly insentient beings. Aristotle carefully distinguished between the inorganic (insentient) and the organic (sentient), and further in the realm of the organic between vegetative, sentient, and rational levels of soul. His true interest lay with the rational level of soul, thus with the human being. The Buddha enlarged upon this interest in and preoccupation with the human by including all sentient beings. All sentient beings were to be saved. Now Dōgen pushes the scope of interest even further, one might say far enough to include anything that is. Once these divisions between sentient and insentient are left behind, possibilities open up to understand green mountains' walking.

If walking stops, buddha ancestors do not appear. If walking ends, the buddha-dharma cannot reach the present. Walking forward does not cease; walking backward does not cease. Walking forward does not obstruct walking backward. Walking backward does not obstruct walking forward. This is called the mountains' flow and the flowing mountains. (98)

The mountains' walking can also be called the "mountains' flowing." It is what the mountain does. What the mountain does, its walking or flowing, enables the Buddha-dharma to reach the present and continue on. The mountains' walking or flowing preserves the Buddha-dharma; without such activity the Buddha-dharma would die out. Whether the walking is forward or backward does not much matter. Both are inevitable. Similarly, when a human being practices, sometimes he advances, sometimes he regresses. This is the way things are. What is important is the practice, free from overpreoccupation with forward or backward.

> Green mountains master walking and eastern mountains master traveling on water. Accordingly, these activities are a mountain's practice. Keeping its own form, without changing body and mind a mountain always practices in every place. Don't slander by saying that a green mountain cannot walk and an eastern mountain cannot travel on water. When your understanding is shallow, you doubt the phrase, "Green mountains are walking." When your learning is immature, you are shocked by the words "flowing mountains." Without fully understanding even the words "flowing water," you drown in small views and narrow understanding. (98–99)

Walking and traveling on water are a mountain's practice. Paradoxically, a mountain keeps its own form, does not change body and mind, and yet always practices in every place. This means that, while not changing its form, a mountain is not bound to that form. Otherwise it could not practice in every place. A mountain's practice can manifest itself everywhere and in every thing. Rationally, we cannot grasp this. But then Dōgen goes on to say that we do not even understand the words "flowing water." We speak of water flowing since that is ordinarily what water is supposed to do. This in no way means that we truly understand water's flowing. The fact that we think we do only blocks any possibility of *questioning* water's flowing. All of our narrow views can be compared to looking through a bamboo tube at a corner in the sky.

Dōgen continues this discussion of the various perspectives for seeing waters and mountains, stating that some beings see water as a jeweled ornament, some as wondrous blossoms; hungry ghosts see it as raging fire or pus and blood, dragons see it as a palace or pavilion. Depending upon their past karma that has resulted in their present kind of birth and form, beings see water as what they desire or fear.

> Thus, the views of all beings are not the same. You should question this matter now. Are there many ways to see one thing, or is it a mistake to see many forms as one thing? You should pursue this beyond the limit of pursuit. Accordingly, endeavors in practice-realization of the way are not limited to one or two kinds. The ultimate realm has one thousand kinds and ten thousand ways.
>
> When we think about the meaning of this, it seems that there is water for various beings but there is no original water—there is no water common to all types of beings. (102)

With this passage Dōgen wipes out all traditional ways of viewing the world. One thing is not to be seen in many ways, nor are we to reduce many forms to one thing. Returning to his discussion of water, he then states that there is no original, primal water that is differentiated into various forms; there is no water common to all types of beings under which they could be subsumed. All our modes of classification fail us here. Dōgen's advice is simple: pursue this matter beyond the limits of pursuit. The fact that there is no intellectual solution to those *aporias* makes little difference.

You should know that even though all things are liber-
ated and not tied to anything, they abide in their own
phenomenal expression. However, when most human beings see water they only see that it flows unceasingly. This
is a limited human view; there are actually many kinds of
flowing. Water flows on the earth, in the sky, upward and
downward. It can flow around a single curve or into
many bottomless abysses. When it rises it becomes
clouds. When it descends it forms abysses. (102–3)

This passage is intelligible even to common sense. If we stop
to think about water, we realize that it is not confined to rivers
and streams, but goes beneath the earth into abysses and rises to
the heavens to become clouds. Our own bodies are largely made
up of water; here we have a different kind of "flowing." Even
though all things, all forms are not bound to anything specific,
they abide in their own dharma-situations. They cannot be
equated with that dharma-situation, but they abide there. Thus, a
certain *stasis* is achieved in the world of impermanence.

A final quote should suffice to convey Dōgen's insistence on
leaving ordinary human thinking and experiencing behind. Perhaps he is unique in this effort, not only to reach some "authentic"
kind of experience, but to abandon any human viewpoint whatsoever. We have an emphasis on authenticity in nineteenth- and
twentieth-century "existential" philosophers such as Søren
Kierkegaard, Jean-Paul Sartre, Gabriel-Honoré Marcel, and Martin
Heidegger. But there seems to be no precedent, at least in the West,
for an absolutely nonanthropomorphic way of experiencing.

If you do not learn to be free from your superficial views,
you will not be free from the body and mind of an ordinary person. Then you will not understand the land of
Buddha ancestors, or even the land or palace of ordinary
people.

Now human beings well know as water what is in the ocean and what is in the river, but they do not know what dragons and fish see as water and use as water. Do not foolishly suppose that what we see as water is used as water by all other beings. You who study with buddhas should not be limited to human views when you are studying water. You should study how you view the water used by buddha ancestors. You should study whether there is water or no water in the house of buddha ancestors. (104)

We have extracted for our discussion mainly passages emphasizing a nonanthropomorphic way of viewing the world. There are many other bold and baffling thoughts in this extraordinary fascicle that cannot be discussed here.

Transformation of Person Into Formless Self

Having attempted to follow Dōgen in his exploration of nonanthropological perspectives, we once again turn to the question of what he means by "self." To begin with, self cannot be equated with person. In the fascicle entitled "Only Buddha knows Buddha" (Yuibutsu Yobutsu), the self that Dōgen is talking about is the self that has attained realization; it is by no means the ordinary self.

Buddha-dharma cannot be known by a person. For this reason, since olden times no ordinary person has realized Buddha-dharma; no practitioner of the Lesser Vehicles has mastered Buddha-dharma. Because it is realized by buddhas alone, it is said, "Only buddha knowing buddha can thoroughly master it. When you realize Buddha-dharma, you do not think, "This is realization just as I expected." Even if you think so, realization invariably differs from your expectation. Realization is not like your conception of it. Accordingly, realization cannot take place as previously conceived. When you realize Buddha-dharma, you do not consider how realization came about. You should reflect on this: What you think one way or another before realization is not a help for realization.[43]

Our customary mode of experiencing has nothing to do with realization. Not only is it not a help; it is a direct hindrance. An abrupt break in experiencing comes about. Thus, upon realization I cannot think; this is what I thought it would be. Even if I did think this way, it would only be a delusion. Realization cannot be conceptualized or anticipated. As Heidegger and others with him emphasized, human being is future-oriented. This is particularly the case with Western man in the Judeo-Christian tradition. It need not have anything to do with religion. Marx is as future-oriented as Hegel. Sartre's example of looking for Pierre in the café is quite apt here. I am looking for, anticipating Pierre; everything else in view is phased out.

A rather pallid example of this break in experiencing can be seen when we suddenly encounter someone we did not expect to see, someone out of context. For a moment we are startled, and our experiencing stops short; there is a complete breach of continuity. If we reflect upon this, the enormous role that anticipation and projecting play in our experience might dawn upon us.

However, it is worth noticing that what you think one way or another is not a help for realization Then you are cautious not to be small-minded. If realization came forth by the power of your prior thoughts, it would not be trustworthy. Realization does not depend on thoughts, but comes forth far beyond them; realization is helped only by the power of realization itself. Know that then there is no delusion and there is no realization.[44]

The matter at stake here is a bit tricky. In the paragraph preceding this passage, Dōgen stated that past thoughts in themselves were clearly realization. It appears contradictory, at least initially, to say that realization has nothing to do with past thoughts and then to say that past thoughts are in themselves realization. However, the contradiction disappears when it becomes clear that past thoughts, all thoughts, and thinking in general, are obscured and marred by habit; they are deluded. But for Dōgen delusion has no ultimate reality. Thus, past thoughts were actually realization, realization that we were unable to realize. A parallel can be found in Dōgen's discussion of being-time; everything is being-time, regardless of whether we realize it or not.

If realization could be produced by the power of prior thought, we could never be certain that it was realization. It would remain forever "mental," wishful thinking. Realization does not depend on what we interpret as our thoughts; it comes from beyond our conscious experience. This does not mean that it comes from the unconscious. It simply does not come from us, from the structure of our conscious or unconscious minds.

The last sentence of this passage appears more puzzling than it actually is. If realization is all there is, it makes no sense to speak of realization, and one certainly cannot speak of delusion.

> Not to know what it is like on this buddha's path is fool-
> ish. What it is like is to be unstained. To be unstained does
> not mean that you try forcefully to exclude intention or
> discrimination. Being unstained cannot be intended or
> discriminated at all.
>
> Being unstained is like meeting a person and not con-
> sidering what he looks like. Also it is like not wishing for
> more color or brightness when viewing flowers or the
> moon. Spring has the tone of spring, and autumn has the
> scene of autumn, there is no escaping it. So if you want
> spring or autumn to be different from what it is, notice
> that it can only be as it is. Or when you want to keep
> spring or autumn as it is, reflect that it has no unchanging
> nature.[45]

Dōgen does not use "being unstained" in any moralistic sense of purity. Rather, it is a state or disposition free of preconceptions and what Nietzsche called "wishful thinking."[46] Both preconceptions and wishful thinking block any direct experience of "reality" as it is. In this passage, preconceptions are primarily related to meeting someone. Being unstained here means not categorizing someone or comparing him with others. In general, comparison can be an unfruitful enterprise. For example, if I constantly compare myself with others, this is actually irrelevant to what I am. There is always someone "better" than I, always someone "worse." What is important is the uniqueness of what I am or what someone is.

Wishful thinking, not Dōgen's phrase, is perhaps more widespread. We all know what we like and do not like. We want flowers to have more color, the moon more brightness. We wish spring were autumn or vice versa, or we wish that spring would always remain spring. Although for Dōgen spring does not turn into summer, yet it has no unchanging nature and cannot remain indefinitely. Things simply are as they are, regardless of what we want or do not want. Being unstained cannot be intended or wished for at all. It has to occur of itself.

> That which is accumulated is without self, and no mental activity has self. The reason is that not one of the four great elements or the five skandhas can be understood as self or identified as self. Therefore, the form of the flowers or moon in your mind should not be understood as being self, even though you think it is self. Still, when you clarify that there is nothing to be disliked or longed for, then the original face is revealed by your practice of the way.[47]

Buddhism analyzes the human being in various ways. The four great elements and five skandhas are two of the classifications generated by this analysis. But whereas earlier (Theravada) Buddhism states that the classifications are what we are and that there is therefore no such thing as self (*anatman*) in the Hindu sense, Dōgen is saying that self is none of these classifications, thereby implying that there is "something else," that is, the original face. This passage states that there are three interrelated factors which are not self: that which is accumulated, our habitual mode of relating to the world; our mental activity; the form of objects in our mind. One might add an emphasis on the first skandha, rupaskandha, the sensuous or the body with which many people tend to equate themselves. For example, seeing is nothing that I *do*; it occurs. It does not belong (exclusively) to me; it is not mine.

> Also learn that the entire universe is the dharma body of the self. To seek to know the self is invariably the wish of living beings. However, those who see the true self are rare. Only buddhas know the true self.
>
> People outside the way regard what is not self as the self. But what buddhas call the self is the entire universe. Therefore, there is never an entire universe that is not the self, with or without knowing it.[48]

Stated simply, the basic problem here is that people regard what is not the self as the self. There exists something that can be called the "true self," but it has nothing to do with ego, person, mental activity, or the habitual accumulation that we normally understand as personal identity. Dōgen's true self is cosmic; it is the entire universe. This holds true regardless of whether we know it or not. As Dōgen states later in the fascicle, the way is not a matter of our knowing or now knowing. As far as knowing or not knowing, understanding or not understanding go, they are like the seasons. They do not hinder each other or turn into each other. At one time there is understanding; at another there is no understanding.

Again turning to the nonanthropological dimensions of self, Dōgen discusses fish, birds, and beasts, stating that they, unlike people, know one another's hearts. A bird can see traces of all sorts of birds in the sky, whereas beasts cannot even conceive of this. We would probably be prone to classify this fact under "instinct." Animals have more developed senses and instincts than humans. But the word "instinct" hardly clarifies how this can be so. Dōgen is speaking about some sort of eye which can see directly inside, as it were. He then transposes this to apply to buddhas.

> Again when a bird flies in the sky, beasts do not even dream of finding or following its trace. As they do not know that there is such a thing, they cannot even imagine this. However, a bird can see traces of hundreds and thousands of small birds having passed in flocks, or traces of so many lines of large birds having flown south or north. These traces may be even more evident than the carriage tracks left on a road or the hoofprints of a horse in the grass. In this way, a bird sees birds' traces.
>
> Buddhas are like this. You may wonder how many lifetimes buddhas have been practicing. Buddhas, large or small, although they are countless, all know their own traces. You never know a buddha's trace when you are not a buddha.
>
> You may wonder why you do not know. The reason is that, while buddhas see these traces with a buddha's eye, those who are not buddhas do not have a buddha's eye, and just notice the buddha's attributes.[49]

Just noticing the buddha's attributes is the opposite of being unstained; it is viewing a buddha from the outside. Knowing traces, whether this be birds knowing other birds or buddhas knowing buddhas, is a matter of direct, immediate "knowing" or sensing. Traces have undeniably to do with the past, with what has already been and is thus actual and real. The fact that Buddhahood is possible is attested by its already being in actuality. Dōgen admonishes us to illuminate our trace by studying the Buddha's trace.

Dialogues with Tillich

In order to facilitate understanding of ideas quite foreign to our Western way of thinking, a perusal of the dialogues between Paul Tillich and Shin'ichi Hisamatsu may be able to open some doors. In these dialogues the Eastern viewpoint is mediated and also often challenged by the Western one. Thus, that Eastern viewpoint is, so to speak, filtered through a westerner's attempt to understand it instead of simply being starkly presented without that mediation or filter. This may not be the most "pure" approach, but it is a beginning.

I

Beginning with a discussion of how to find a degree of calmness in the midst of a busy life, the dialogue moves to the question of what it is that enables us to find that calm. Hisamatsu states that this is awakening to the "Calm" or "True Self." This self is at work, for example, when Tillich is busily preparing his lectures while traveling on trains. Tillich then asks whether this self must be conscious or possess a kind of psychological awareness. Hisamatsu replies that this awareness is not psychological, nor is it even a state of mind; rather, it is No-Consciousness or No-Mind. Mindful of the contemporary efforts to get beyond the subject-object split in consciousness, Tillich asks whether that is what is accomplished in No-Mind. Hisamatsu answers that the subject-object split is not present in No-Mind, but that does not exhaust the matter; nor does No-Mind entail going to some other realm. Hisamatsu then takes up his own term for No-Mind, that is, the "Formless Self."

With that we have arrived at the source of the title of this study. After scrutinizing the three dialogues between Tillich and Hisamatsu, we shall try to further elucidate what kind of "self" this Formless Self could be. It has little to do with what we ordinarily associate with the term "self."

In keeping with the Zen rejection of metaphysical speculation and its preference for the concrete, Hisamatsu gives the illustration of the functioning of our eyes. When the eyes function properly and naturally, there is not consciousness of seeing.

> If the seer is consciously aware of seeing—for instance, this glass of orange juice—then that is not pure seeing. . . . In pure seeing, however, in which the duality between the seer and the seen is overcome, the orange juice in a sense "disappears." It is there; yet it is not. It is this sort of "disappearance of mind" that is meant by "No-Mind" or "No-Mindedness." When one is conscious of what one is doing, you can speak of a state of mind; for the mind remains."[1]

What can it mean to say that in pure seeing the orange juice in a sense disappears? Beyond saying that the orange juice disappears as an object separated from the seeing subject (no subject-object split), what is the "positive" content of such a statement? What does it mean to see a glass of orange juice not as an object? This can perhaps be better illustrated by an example from the realm of hearing that by its nature has less to do with objects; as in the case of music, for instance, it has nothing to do with objects at all.

The example consists of listening to a bell, a gong, perhaps in a Zendo. If one listens in a certain, that is, a "pure" and noncon-

ceptual way, one does not hear a bell; one hears vibrations opening out into space, gradually receding into silence. One knows it
is a bell, but one does not hear a bell; one hears vibrations, one
hears vibrat*ing*. This is pure hearing. One is not thinking: that is a
bell; what kind of bell or gong is it? This cluster of questions and
opinions that usually accompany our experience is what is meant
by "mind" here. Therefore, pure hearing is No-Mind or the activity of the Formless Self.

Pure hearing and pure seeing are beyond the dichotomy of
hearing and not hearing, seeing and not seeing. There is a well
known precedent for this with regard to thinking.

> After sitting, a monk asked Great Teacher Yueh-shan
> Hung-tao: "What are you thinking of in the immobile
> state of sitting?"
> The master replied: "I think of not-thinking." The
> monk asked: "How can you think of not thinking?"
> The master replied: "By non-thinking."[2]

Since seeing and hearing are more tangible and thus perhaps
more accessible than thinking, they might be able to facilitate our
concrete understanding of what it means to be beyond the dichotomy of seeing and not seeing, being, and nonbeing. The dialogue does not help us here since Hisamatsu states that there is a
consciousness beyond seeing and not seeing, and Tillich says he
understands that to a certain extent and immediately shifts back
to his existential question of how to find calm in the midst of
busyness.

What could a seeing that is beyond the dualism of seeing and
not seeing be like? An initial, easy answer is that this kind of seeing would not see objects. Then what is seen? A presence. Not a
static object, but a dynamic, vibrant presencing. This is perhaps
most evident in certain paintings or drawings of landscapes,
Western, and Eastern. Chinese landscape drawings hardly depict
objects. They largely present emptiness offset by some kind of

marginal figure, perhaps a figure with a large hat crossing a bridge, or a sprig of blossoms, or a bird perched on a branch. Hisamatsu's book *Zen and the Fine Arts* has eloquent instances of such landscapes. For him, they present the Formless Self.

In such instances one sees *through* and *beyond* ordinary seeing. One sees the form of the Formless Self. If the form were not there, one could not see the Formless Self. And yet the Formless Self cannot simply be equated with some particular form of an object.

Pursuing Tillich's question about how to find calm in the midst of busyness, the dialogue moves to a discussion of Meister Eckhart's *Abgeschiedenheit*. Tillich translates *Abgeschiedenheit* as "separatedness." Actually, one could add to this the emphasis on *Abschied*, taking leave of something or someone. Thus, "separating" in the sense of taking leave or bidding farewell might be more appropriate than separatedness which can have the implication that something has always been statically separated and distinct.

Hisamatsu shifts the emphasis in *Abgeschiedenheit* to a total emptying of all things, which is closer to the verbal sense of separating. Yet what separates is indeed empty of that from which it separates, but not yet necessarily totally empty of all things.

Tillich then describes his own meditative life which involves concentrating on the subject matter of his speeches, lectures, or sermons, whether it be traveling on trains or sitting in a café. Hisamatsu replies that concentration on something is still concentration on an object by a subject. What he means by "concentration" must be objectless and subjectless. Both object and subject in a sense simply cease "to be," and all there is is nondualistic concentration.

The crux of the final impossibility of complete agreement between Tillich and Hisamatsu centers finally on the issue of form versus formless. Tillich speaks of the spark, the seed, the *logos* that Eckhart finds in every man of which he does not empty himself. This *logos* is basically potentiality.

The *logos*. But this is not the formless. The *logos* is the form of God, which is born. The actualization is often called by him "being born." The *logos* is being born in us; Christ is again born through us, as is Mary, symbolically speaking. This is not the Formless Self.[3]

The issue at stake here is whether awakening to the Formless Self can ultimately be described in terms of a development from potentiality to actuality. Since there "is" no Formless Self until it has been awakened to, strictly speaking the awakening cannot be described as a development from potentiality to actuality. This is a subtle, but important point. The Formless Self in a state of potentiality does not exist. This developmental process from potentiality to actuality with regard to Buddha-nature had already been emphatically rejected by Dōgen.

Hisamatsu then introduces the term *Armut*, poverty. The component "*Mut*" in the German term decidedly indicates that a "mental" or spiritual poverty is meant as opposed to any kind of material poverty. Tillich immediately defines complete poverty as the emptying of the subject-object duality. Somehow this does not quite satisfy Hisamatsu. We need to take a look at what Eckhart actually says about this matter which is related to several similar terms including "*Gelassenheit*" and "*Lassen*," releasement and letting go.

It is in this manner, I declare, that a man should be so acquitted and free that he neither knows nor realizes that God is at work in him: in that way can a man possess poverty. The masters say God is a being, an intellectual being that knows all things. But we say God is not a being and not intellectual and does not know this or that. Thus, God is free of all things, so He is all things.[4]

Poverty means to be unaware that God is at work within a self. God himself is not *a* being and does not know this or that.

Not being himself a being and not knowing things, he is free or empty of all things and is thus free to *be* (transitive) them.

Eckhart states that a poor man *wills* nothing, *knows* nothing, and possesses nothing. Then a statement follows that appears to have escaped Tillich:

> I have often said, and eminent authorities say it too, that a man should be so free of all things and all works, both inward and outward, that he may be a proper abode for God where God can work. Now we shall say something else. If it is the case that a man is free of all creatures, of God and of self, and if it is still the case that God finds a place *in him* to work, then we declare that as long as this is *in* that man, he is not poor with the strictest poverty. For it is not God's intention in His works that a man should have a place within himself for God to work in: for poverty of spirit means being so free of God and all His works, that God, if he wishes to work in the soul, is Himself the place where he works—and this he gladly does.[5]

In contrast to Eckhart, for whom complete poverty means not simply removing the subject-object dualism, but being free of everything including God, Tillich insists that the *logos* remains in us and mediates everything that happens in our work. Tillich can speak of a divine abyss from which we come, but the mediation of the *logos* is always present. Hisamatsu counters that the divine abyss is not that from which the self or concrete thing comes; the abyss *is* the self or the concrete thing. Otherwise there is a duality between the abyss and the self or concrete thing. Harboring the characteristic Western aversion to the formless traceable back to the ancient Greeks, Tillich tries to maintain the ultimate individuality of form.

> But he [Eckhart] would emphasize the *logos* and love doctrine, which gives to the form, to the special form—to this

liquid here—the power of being which in this moment is not swallowed by the Formless Self.[6]

Hisamatsu then states that Tillich is still maintaining a dualism between the Formless Self and the liquid. Form is not swallowed or threatened by the Formless Self. That would make the Formless Self into some sort of a being. Because of the working of the Formless Self, things with form are able to emerge.

This first dialogue concludes with a discussion of art, a realm of special significance to both Tillich and Hisamatsu. Hisamatsu states that an artist who has awakened to his Formless Self expresses that Formless Self in his painting. If such a painting is observed by another Formless Self, the experience allows the observer to deepen his understanding of his own Formless Self. Tillich states emphatically that this is not possible. One can only say "deepen beyond his empirical self to the dimension of the other self." While not denying this formulation, Hisamatsu states that "beyond" and "other" does not exhaustively characterize the matter. They still contain traces of duality.

II

The second dialogue begins with Tillich's question to Hisamatsu: how does he couple artistic form with the Formless Self? Hisamatsu's initial answer is that since it is self, the Formless Self includes self-awareness and is active in expressing or presenting itself through artistic form. Tillich focuses his question on the content of, for example, a particular painting. Hisamatsu's reply is that what is expressing itself in the painting is always the Formless Self. This Formless Self can express itself in anything; thus, it may be said to have boundless contents. Tillich then states that content would mean, for example, the sea, the mountain or the landscape. Hisamatsu denies this, stating that mountains and rivers, or flowers and birds constitute the *Moment* for the Formless Self to express itself. Zen art has nothing to do with a realistic copying of natural phenomena. The discussion then centers on the meaning of the German word, *Moment*, which was crucial for Hegel's dialectic. A *Moment* can be understood either temporally, in which case its meaning is identical with that of the English word "moment," or else it can be understood structurally as a special kind of factor or catalyst. The latter sense is primarily intended here. Tillich's conception of *kairos,* the ripe time, is now introduced as being close to what is meant by *Moment.* One is reminded of Brutus' speech in Shakespeare's *Julius Caesar.*

> There is a tide in the affairs of men,
> Which taken at the flood, leads on to fortune;
> Omitted, all the voyage of their life
> Is bound in shallows and in miseries.
> On such a full sea are we now afloat;
> And we must take the current when it serves,
> Or lose our ventures.[7]

The only difference, but a crucial one, is that Brutus is talking about deciding to take action at a favorable time, *carpe diem,* whereas the *Moment,* the right condition or occasion, triggers an awakening in the Zen student that is not a matter of any conscious decision. The student just wakes up to his Formless Self.

> The mark of Zen aesthetic appreciation, accordingly, is to see within form what is formless—which means to see in things with form the Self-Without-Form.[8]

We can only see the Formless Self within form, since forms are always what we see.

Tillich finds in Hisamatsu's remarks an affinity with what he calls "the depth of being" in things. For both thinkers art transmits something beyond itself: for Tillich this leads to God as the ultimate source of being; for Hisamatsu it leads to man's true or Formless Self.

The discussion now leads out of the realm of art into that of religion itself. Hisamatsu finds the ground of and need for religion in the fact that human being not only has, but is, an ultimate antimony. The interpreter, Richard De Martino, answers for Hisamatsu:

> For Dr. Hisamatsu it is the dualistic opposition between the positive and the negative: existentially (or, if the term is permissible, "onto-existentially"), between being and nonbeing; axiologically between the good and the "not-good"—or evil—in the sphere of morals, the beautiful and the unbeautiful in aesthetics, and the true and the untrue in the dominion of the cognitive.[9]

Tillich's own view of the ground of and need for religion, its raison d'être, lies in the experience of belonging to the Infinite and of being excluded from it at the same time. The goal of religion is thus reunion with the Infinite. This reunion is available to us only in a fragmentary way; total reunion can only be anticipated. Hisamatsu replies:

> What I would like to speak of, however, is not a fragmentary, anticipatory overcoming, but a fundamental resolution that goes down to the root. For the ultimate antimony can be resolved only at its root, that is why it cannot be dealt with either by cognitive-learning, morality, or art. Still, to solve this problem that reason cannot solve there must be a solution that will nevertheless satisfy reason. That is, although the problem cannot be solved by "rationality," as it is an affliction of the "rational" or "human" being, every such being has the inevitable desire to solve it. Thus it is that the proper concern of religion is no other than to resolve this ultimate antinomy.[10]

For both thinkers there is an ultimate antinomy in human existence, an antinomy most fundamentally expressed by life-death and being-nonbeing. Tillich even nonorthodoxically accepts nonbeing or evil, in God, but only potentially, never actually. Such a position betrays the influence of Schelling's *On Human Freedom,* perhaps the philosophical treatise that most honestly attempts to deal with the question of evil.

Tillich sees reconciliation or reunion of the finite with the infinite by way of fragmentary anticipation in this historical existence, with final resolution being achieved in eternity. Hisamatsu, on the other hand, wishes to resolve the ultimate antinomy at its root, not fragmentarily and not by way of anticipation, but by way of radically and existentially confronting the antinomy that then opens up the direction toward eternity. The *Moment* or catalyst for resolving the antinomy lies in doubting or the Great Doubt Block which is an actualization of the ultimate antinomy embodied in the one who doubts.

Tillich then asks if the resolution of the ultimate antinomy is not by anticipation, is it in time and space? Hisamatsu's reply is that in this breakthrough there is no time and space and if it were no more than temporal and spatial, it could not be said to be conclusive. Tillich then objects that the awakening happened to Hisamatsu, not to his shoemaker or to Hitler. Hisamatsu states that the Formless Self has neither a beginning, an ending, a special place, or a special time. Tillich immediately replies that then it cannot happen to a human being. De Martino states that the Great Death entails at once a Great Birth beyond birth and death and that the one to whom that happened in one sense ceases to "be." Further discussion is basically unable to get beyond this impasse and the dialogue soon concludes.

III

The third and last dialogue begins with a brief discussion of freedom. With regard to the painting of *Dancing Pu-tai,* Hisamatsu states that the predominant Zen quality in this work is unattached freedom. To the inquiry what it is that the figure is free from, Hisamatsu replies freedom from everything, and De Martino explicates:

> It is, of course, not alone a "freedom from." Rooted in the Self that is Not-of-form—or, in your designation, "Being itself"—it enjoys the unlimited "freedom to" realize its self-expression in any form. . . .
>
> Though I used your term, "Being itself," actually it is not confined to being—nor, for that matter, to nonbeing. In fact, the justification for characterizing it as "unconditioned" is exactly that it is free of the duality of "being-and-nonbeing." This is the reason Zen does not speak of "Being itself," which is still in some sort of conflict with "nonbeing."[11]

Here we see the difficulty Hisamatsu has with Tillich's Being itself. In contrast to the Formless Self, which Hisamatsu asserts to be beyond the opposition of form-formless, Being itself still stands in dualistic opposition to nonbeing. Hisamatsu then states that Zen is unattached to anything, including Buddha and especially unattachment itself. This is an important point. First of all, "unattachment" is a better term for the more common "detachment" which tends to be construed as having nothing to do with something, as total indifference. Second, one can get insidiously attached to the idea of unattachment, just as one can take great pride in being humble or modest. If one is attached to the idea of freedom, one can hardly be said to be free. Consequently, what is needed is a freedom that is free of the duality of freedom-unfreedom.

Tillich comes back to the main objection he has been raising throughout all the dialogue: that the *specific* form of *Dancing Putai* must have an inner relationship to ultimate reality or the Formless Self. Ultimate formlessness and the finite form must be related in some way. Hisamatsu replies that in its self-concretization the Formless Self can assume innumerable forms. Tillich persists in thinking the Formless Self is somehow separate from the specific forms in which it manifests itself. But the point is that the Formless Self does not have any form apart from the specific forms in which it manifests itself. Apart from the specific forms, the Formless Self "is" not. Tillich then says one specific form would stand absolutely for the ultimate, and this would preclude all other specific forms. De Martino then amends Tillich's "stand for" to read "ex-presses." A specific form does not stand for or represent the ultimate; the ultimate is ex-pressed, literally pressed out or injected into, the specific form.

What Tillich is unable to understand or accept is that one expression or form is not the exclusive manifestation of the Formless Self, shutting out any other manifestations. The Formless Self can manifest itself in any form. And yet any one expression or form expresses the ultimate *entirely*. It is not a partial manifestation, but a *total* one.

Still persevering with his main objection, Tillich mentions that in Hisamatsu's book *Zen and the Fine Arts* there are over a hundred individual representations of ultimate reality. The fact that he adheres to the term "representation" shows that he did not grasp the distinction between representation and expression. When something represents or stands for the ultimate, the ultimate is not present in it; the ultimate remains apart and absent. But when the ultimate is ex-pressed in something, it is present in it. The ultimate *is* the specific form. Apart from being a specific form, the ultimate "is" not.

De Martino tries to satisfy Tillich's concern over preserving the particular by stating that nothing is ever reduced to any other thing. In saying "I am thou," the "I" does not cancel out the "thou." That would be what Buddhism calls a "false sameness," a flat identity in which particularity is annihilated. Thus, formlessness never swallows up particularity; that would simply be vague, vacuous formlessness. This is not what Zen is talking about. Rather, Zen aims for true individuality. Tillich asks what that phrase means. Hisamatsu replies.

Ordinary individuals are unfulfilled, isolated, or disinte-
grated, and cannot be regarded as authentic individuals.
Authentic individuality as understood in Zen Buddhism
may be explained in terms of the Hua-yen concept of "*jiji-
muge*" (the nonobstruction between particular and particular) or the T'ien t'ai concept of "*koko-enjō*" (each
individual fulfilled). A particular or individual of this
order would be "genuinely" individual.[12]

As an example of the nonobstruction between or interpenetration of particular and particular, De Martino states, "I am the
flower." Tillich objects that such paradoxical statements cannot be
realized directly, and De Martino retorts that they can only be realized directly. What Tillich is understandably having difficulty
with is how I am the flower, and yet I remain I and the flower remains the flower. There is no barrier or hindrance between particular and particular, and yet nothing swallows up anything else.
Beginning to get an inkling, Tillich asks whether there is no centered self that would be a hindrance. De Martino replies that the
barrier is created by the reflectively self-conscious ego which discriminates itself dualistically from "not itself." The ego must die
to itself as ego and become the self that is also "Not-Itself" or the
Formless Self. This constitutes the complete fulfillment of the particular. Through the incorporation of its own negation the particular becomes a nonparticular-particular or, in a way, a kind of
"universal." This is the basic meaning of the Diamond Sutra's for-
mulations: A is not-A, therefore A is really A. When A encom-
passes its own negation, there is nothing that stands opposed to
it. A can encompass its own negation because ultimately it *is* not-
A; it is the Formless Self.

Tillich then says that he must try with his dualistic mind to
understand how the particular or individual is simultaneously
preserved and not preserved. He could understand if the particular were said to be transparent or translucent to another particular. De Martino replies:

Were "translucency" or "transparency" to mean "emptiness" or "Formlessness," that might be acceptable. Because to Dr. Hisamatsu—or to Zen—it would not be
"transparent" or "translucent" for "anything-else," for
anything "other-to-it." Just the opposite, "transparency"
and "translucency" would rather denote the "nondualis-
tically ecstatic" "absence-in presence"—or "presence-
absence"—of its own "Self-Negation-Fulfillment."[13]

What can it mean that something is transparent, not for something other, but for itself? Instead of allowing something other to
shine through it, the thing shines out of itself so to speak. It ecsta-
tically empties itself, and in negating its own substantial form, it
fulfills itself. The "structure" of self-emptying is fundamentally
and profoundly ecstatic.

Corresponding to the false sameness that annihilates particularity mentioned earlier in the dialogue, Hisamatsu now brings up
a false differentiation or a false individuality, one that absolutizes
itself existing in isolation completely separated from everything
else. Identity alone will not do; difference alone will not do either.

The discussion now turns to the question of the ordinary existence's need to reach the ultimate or Formless Self, thus com-
pleting and fulfilling itself.

"Wanting" the actualization of its ultimate ground or fulfillment, the ordinary has to overcome—or to "negate"
—itself; as the manifold substantialization—or "production"—of its ultimate ground, on the other hand, it becomes a positive "affirmation."[14]

In negating itself, the ordinary achieves a positive affirmation. As long as something has not gotten outside itself, it is incomplete and unfulfilled. Once it has achieved this, it can be
contained in itself. Once it has gotten outside of itself, negated,
and emptied itself of any taint of substantiality, the Formless Self

can see itself in that thing and in any other thing that has gone outside of itself, emptied and negated itself.

We are now facing the limitations of these dialogues, points on which Christianity and Buddhism cannot reach total unanimity. For Zen, the claim is that man can escape the situation of finitude by himself becoming Buddha or the ultimate. In spite of the nontraditional elements in his position, as a Christian, Tillich cannot embrace this possibility. Tillich's "mysticism" remained what he called it, a "nature mysticism"; the union was with nature, not with God. Actually, union is a word that Tillich rejected, preferring the more cautious term "participation."

Returning to the discussion of Hua-yen, Tillich's position remains on the level of *riji-muge*, no obstruction between universal and particular, whereas Zen moves on to the level of *jiji-muge*, no obstruction between particular and particular. The universal is lacking. Every particular is fulfilled and every particular is comprehended within every other.

The formulation between universal and particular no obstruction generates the view of a universal apart from the particular. For this reason Hisamatsu prefers the expression "nonparticular" (negation of the particular) over universal. On the basis of the nonduality of any thing and its own negation rests the nonduality of any thing and any other thing. Thus, each thing "is" and is "in" every other thing.

The discussion now centers on the meaning of this "is," a point touched upon previously. For Tillich, "is" indicates participation. Everything participates in and is an expression of the ultimate. In contrast, for Zen each thing is a *Self*-expression of ultimacy. Tillich's reply is that speaking for himself, he would be shy to say this. The two thinkers seem to have come as close to each other as they are able; of necessity a final difference remains. For Tillich the relation of the particular to the ultimate is that of participation; for Hisamatsu it is nonduality.

Trying to grasp the Zen point of view, Tillich proffers the statement that whereas a dialectical identification of the particular with the ultimate is possible, a direct or immediate identification is not. Hisamatsu replies that he is not speaking about identity. De Martino explicates.

> For, to re-emphasize, it is this "nonduality of itself" and "not itself" (*riji-muge*) that includes as one dimension the "nonduality of itself" and every "other to itself" (*jiji-muge*). *Jiji-muge* is not, therefore, an identification of "two" as "one." It is, rather, the nonduality of two that "are" two even as they cease to be "two" because they in a sense indeed cease to be.[15]

The discussion waxes more concrete again and comes to center on a flower as an example of the particular. Tillich remarks that the flower speaks for him with a magnificent eloquence. Nevertheless, it cannot be for him anything more than a particular. He cannot refer to it as being itself the ultimate. Hisamatsu replies that only when the flower is seen as formless even while formed does the full beauty of the flower emerge. Only when the person gazing at the flower becomes himself formless can the duality between him and the flower, between subject and object, be overcome. The person becomes the flower concentrating on the flower. De Martino elucidates.

> Given your understanding of a particular in contradistinction to a universal in which it participates . . . the idea of a particular incorporating its own negation—that is, being "formless," and thereby incorporating every "other" particular (*jiji-muge*) may be somewhat forbidding. In any case, it may make clear why I said before that whereas for you the ultimate—or "God"—finally remains transcendent, for Zen, as there "is" no universal besides the particular fulfilled in and through its own Self-Negation (which is thus a Self-Negation-Affirmation), there isn't any such predominantly transcendent ultimate.[16]

De Martino elaborates on this by saying that with Zen what may be spoken of as "universal" is the lack of any interposition between particular and particular. This pretty much concludes the substance of the dialogues.

Oriental Nothingness

In the hope of throwing additional light on these difficult questions, we now take a brief look at an article of Hisamatsu's entitled "The Characteristics of Oriental Nothingness," plus a few remarks from some of his other writings.

In an attempt to get at what is unique about oriental nothingness, Hisamatsu enumerates five meanings of nothingness. Anyone who finds this odd or even absurd should be reminded that the rationalist Kant listed four different meanings of nothingness. "The talk of this division of the concept of *nothing* would therefore have to be drawn up as follows:

Nothing,
as

1
Empty concept without object
ens rationis

2
Empty object of a concept
nihil privativum

3
Empty intuition without
object *ens imaginarius*

4
Empty object without concept
nihil negativum[17]

Kant, of course, investigates the question of the nothing within the framework of his conception of knowledge as necessarily composed of concepts and intuitions. Given his statement that thoughts without content are empty, intuitions without concepts are blind,[18] we are told that knowledge has to be composed of both elements, intuition and concept. Ordered under the guidance of the categories, nothing in accordance with quantity is an entity of reason, *ens rationis,* an example of which is the noumenon. I can *think* the noumenon, indeed for Kant I must think it; but I cannot *know* it since I cannot intuit it. Nothing according to quality is privative, *nihil privativum,* examples of which are shadow as a privation or lack of light and cold as a privation or lack of heat. Nothing according to the category of relation is an entity of the imagination, *ens imaginarium,* examples of which are the pure forms of sensibility, space, and time. Finally, nothing according to the category of modality is *nihil negativum,* negative nothingness, examples of which are a square circle or a two-sided rectilinear figure. Since these are contradictions, this last meaning of the nothing cannot be said to exist at all, whereas the other three in some sense "exist."

However, the framework within which Kant investigates the meanings of the nothing is very strict and very much unique to him. Thus, it cannot be of much assistance in our inquiry. It was cited in order to show that there are various possible meanings for the nothing and various ways to think about it. It is far from being merely a vacuous idea.

Hisamatsu's listing is quite different from that of Kant.

1. Nothingness as the negation of being
   Example: There is no desk; there is no pleasure.
2. Nothingness as a predicative negation
   Examples: A desk is not a chair; pleasure is not grief.
3. Nothingness as an abstract concept—this is nonbeing in general in contrast to being or somethingness in general.
4. Nothingness as a conjecture
   Example: While alive, I imagine myself as dead or nonexisting.

5. Nothingness as absence of consciousness
    Examples: deep sleep, unconsciousness, death.[19]

Hisamatsu then proceeds to state that Oriental Nothingness is different from all these meanings. Fundamentally, Oriental Nothingness is beyond the duality of being and nonbeing. It is also beyond delimitation and predication. It is not a passive, contemplated state, perhaps achieved through "meditation," but rather the active, contemplating mind. It is not something sought for, but rather itself "seeking."

In an effort to get at some sort of "positive" content of Oriental Nothingness, a task bordering or self-contradiction, Hisamatsu investigates the assertion that it is like empty space. He lists the characteristics of empty space as follows: no-obstruction, omnipresence, impartiality, broad and great, formless, purity, stability, voiding-being, voiding-voidness, without obtaining. These characteristics are mostly fairly clear and self-explanatory. Empty space does not get in the way of anything. It is present everywhere. It is neutral, having no preferences. It has no limits or form. It is pure, lacking afflictions. It is stable in that it does not come into being or pass away. Again, it is beyond the opposition of being and nonbeing. Finally, it neither itself clings to anything nor can it be clung to. Then follows an absolutely key statement.

> Oriental Nothingness and empty space do have similar characteristics, and to this extent may seem to be the same thing. But, of course, Oriental Nothingness is not the same as empty space, which has neither awareness nor life. Oriental nothingness is the One who is "always clearly aware." Therefore it is called "Mind," "Self," or the "True Man."[20]

Unlike empty space, Oriental Nothingness is not only living, but possesses mind and self-consciousness. The question for us now becomes: what kind of mind or awareness is at stake here? It cannot coincide with what we ordinarily mean by the term "mind," if we bother at all to think what this word really means. The fact that we have a name or word for something by no means entails the fact that we truly understand it. It simply means that something is familiar enough for us to categorize it.

> I once worked with a man in a legal experiment on the effects of the drug LSD. We were in a relatively barren hospital room. It took me a while to discover that the man was going around the room quietly naming things. "That is a chair," he would say to himself. Under LSD everything had become too lively and a little frightening. He pinned them down and limited their existence by naming them. He might as well have said, "You are *only* a chair." I fear our hanging an identity on the sequential confluence of transcendent experiences does about the same thing. Naming implies that we have comprehended, circumscribed, delimited, put down. Naming the chair doesn't mean I really understand how it is made or what it is. It says, in effect, you are of the class of things I've seen before. Of course self or personal identity is also of the class of things I've seen before—whatever it is.[21]

Probably the word "awareness" could be considered more useful than "mind." Mind (Latin *mens*) somehow conjures up the image of an entity or thing whereas awareness does no such thing. Awareness rather implies the activity of being awake and alert, as is brought out more clearly in the term "wary." Actually, awareness is related to the German term *wahr*, true.

> The nature of Awareness beyond conceptual differentiation is that it directly knows Itself in and through Itself. It is not like ordinary consciousness or knowing, which is a conditioned, object-dependent intentional knowing. It is

not, however, the same as a great hollow emptiness, vacuous and unknowing.[23]

The slightest familiarity with Eastern texts will tell us that we are not dealing with a subject-object structure of mind here. And in contemporary Western thought as well vast efforts are being made to get out of the Cartesian subject-object, mind-body split. But merely to know what is being rejected is not sufficient; we need to sense the direction in which we are moving.

> The True Buddha is not without mind, but possesses Mind which is "without mind and without thought," is not without self-awareness, but possesses Awareness which is "without awareness"—an egoless ego, is not without life, but possesses Life which is ungenerated and unperishing.[23]

As is frequently the case, the customary meaning of a word must be negated in order to arrive at a deeper possibility. All of this has its roots in the well-known formula of the Diamond Sutra: A is not A, therefore A is A. Expressed less abstractly by contemporary interpreters:

> In order to see through true green, true red, one must go through a spiritual transformation, one must go through the phase of negation; pasture is not pasture, red is not red. Then one can truly appreciate the greenness of the pasture and the brilliant redness of a flower.[24]

Returning to Hisamatsu, he further characterizes nothingness as the seeing heart itself. He cites the following exchange between Ta-chu and a monk: "Tell me, how can one see (*schauen*) the Buddha-nature?" "Seeing itself is the Buddha-nature."[25]

Hisamatsu goes on to say that seeing and the heart are not to be separated from each other. If they are, then the true heart and true seeing are no longer present.

The nothingness of Zen does not represent a space, free of objects, outside of my person, but is rather my own state of nothingness, namely my self that is "nothing." (25)

Fully aware of the inappropriateness of an attempt to conceptually present the nothingness of Zen and yet at the same time of the urgency to do so in order to help those seeking it, Hisamatsu struggles with the subject-object structure of Indo-European language (in this case, German). We tend to represent nothingness as "something" outside ourselves. But, of course, nothingness is in no sense of the word a "something," and it is not outside of us. Neither is it "inside" us. We need to get rid of the framework outside-inside. But since the tendency to represent nothingness outside ourselves in more prevalent, Hisamatsu takes the opposite strategic tack and brings nothingness closer to the self.

"There is nothing in me" does not mean that nothing is in my inside, if it is the case that my I is divided into inside and outside; rather, it means that nowhere is there something. . . . Zen-Buddhist nothingness is the nowhere is there something that is I, or conversely: the I that is the nowhere is there something. If one spoke of a nowhere is there something without the I, that would then only be empty space; or if one spoke of an I without the nowhere is there something, this I would only be a psychological or physical phenomenon; but neither can be designated as the nothingness of Zen. (25–26)

Without the I, the nowhere is there something is just empty space; without the nowhere is there something the I is simply encapsulated in its own phantasy with no possibility of *ecstasis,* of getting outside itself. We need both factors or, rather, we need ultimately to get *beyond* both.

Your true nature is like the empty space of the heavens
and if you succeed in seeing the nowhere is there something, that can be called appropriate seeing. (*Hui-neng*)

In Cheng-tao-ko and in Chuan-hsin fa-yao we read:

"Nothingness is clear seeing. It is the nowhere is there
something. It is neither man nor Buddha." (28)

Hisamatsu next takes up the word "emptiness" in an attempt
to further explicate the "nowhere is there something." He cites
Shih-mo-ho-yen-lun who lists ten meanings in his "Dispute over
the Great Vehicle of Buddhism."

First, it is unobstructed. That means that no phenomenon, no matter what its nature, constitutes an obstruction
for it.

Second, it is omnipresent. That means that there is no
place that it does not reach.

Third, it is without distinction. That means that it
knows no distinction.

Fourth, it is open and wide. That means that there is
no limit for it.

Fifth, it is without appearance. That means that it presents no appearance accessible to the senses.

Sixth, it is pure. That means that it is immaculate and
without flaw.

Seventh, it is permanent (*dauernd*) and unmoved.
That means that it is without becoming and perishing.

Eighth, it is empty of being. That means that it is beyond all measure.

Ninth, it is empty without emptiness (*leerelos leer*).
That means that it does not cling to itself.

Tenth, it possesses nothing. That means that it doesn't possess and also cannot be possessed. (31)

The gist of all these characteristics seems to be not only that emptiness is empty; it absolutely *tolerates* no obstruction or impediment. Thus, it can be present anywhere. It refuses to make an appearance, to be accessible to the senses and to be in any way possessed or held on to. It neither comes into being nor passes away in any traditional sense of those terms. It cannot be measured or fathomed, and it doesn't cling to itself.

Reading between the lines, we can suggest that nothingness does not put in an appearance to the senses, but this does not mean that it is totally inaccessible. If it were, all these things could not be stated about it. Thus, we can surmise that it makes itself felt or "sensed" (not perceived with any of the ordinary five senses, but sensed in the way, for example, an animal senses danger) at times to a receptive person.

But the nothingness of Zen Buddhism is by no means something unconscious and unalive as is emptiness; Rather, it is the subject that knows itself "clearly and distinctly." For this reason it is also called "heart," "self," or "the true human being." (34)

Zen nothingness is not subhuman; it is transhuman. Nishitani had taken this issue up in his chapter on the personal and the impersonal in religion where he questioned the validity and limits of attributing "personality" to God, thus reducing him to the human level. At the same time, he emphasized that God must include and transcend the "human."

Back to the manner of "appearance" of nothingness. Not only does it not appear to the senses, it cannot be divided up into individual appearances. Rather, it must be sensed in its unlimited totality temporarily on certain "occasions." It is then not contained in or identical with any of these appearances. It simply "makes use" of them to let itself be known.

> It is also explicable in terms of this characteristic of Zen-Buddhist nothingness that a true Buddha cannot dwell in nirvana; for a nirvana that can be represented as a place does signify blissful rest as opposed to the restlessness of the world; but it is not the true nirvana. (40)

Not even a true Buddha can dwell in absolute nothingness or nirvana. Not only is nothingness not a something; it is not any "place" either. Perhaps the closest analogue to this in Western philosophy is the "place" in Plato's *Phaedo* where he states that the soul after its release from the prison of the body goes to a "place" (*topos*) which, like itself, is noble, pure, and invisible.[26]

Again and again Hisamatsu stresses that there are limitations to the extent to which Zen nothingness can be compared to emptiness. (N.B. He always uses the German word for emptiness, *die Leere*, never the Sanskrit *sūnyatā*). Thus, he stresses the heart-nature of nothingness.

> For the nothingness of Zen is not lifeless like emptiness, but, on the contrary, something quite lively (*lebendig*). It is not only lively, but also has heart and, moreover, is aware of itself.[27]

Having stated this, Hisamatsu reintroduces the analogy of liveliness, heart, and self-awareness with emptiness to ward off all familiar associations with these words. The liveliness, heart, and self-awareness of nothingness all have the characteristics of emptiness.

> Our usual heart is full of complexes and impediments, it is limited in its reach, differentiates and classifies, it is an ap-

pearance, it is flawed, it is subject to becoming and passing away, it knows measure, it is graspable, it has an inside
and an outside and many other things in addition.[28]

What Hisamatsu means by "heart" has little to do with our
customary associations with that word. We take heart to be a
physiological organ pumping and sustaining life. Or we take
heart as the seat of sentiment. Again, we need to try to get beyond
the physiological and the psychological. To gain an inkling of that
dimension, we might begin by comparing it to the mood of a non-
spectacular landscape as seen or depicted by an artist, whether a
painter or a poet. To follow this direction of inquiry, we now turn
to Hisamatsu's work *Zen and the Fine Arts*.

> In the case of Zen painting, then, it is not, as is so often the
> case with other types of painting, that a consciousness not
> free of form (the ordinary self) paints a concrete object;
> nor is it that the ordinary self-with-form tries objectively
> to depict what is without form; nor is it that the self-with-
> out-form depicts an object-with-form; nor is it even that
> the Self-Without-Form objectively paints what is form-
> less. Rather, it is always the Formless Self that is, on each
> and every occasion, the creative subject expressing itself.
> . . . This means, finally, that that which paints is that
> which is painted: that which is painted is that which
> paints.[29]

The key sentence here is that which paints is that which is
painted: the Formless Self. According to Hisamatsu, that Formless Self possesses seven characteristics. We want to take a look at
these characteristics as a way leading to a dimension beyond that
of the physiological or the psychological. These seven are: asymmetry, simplicity, austere sublimity or lofty dryness, naturalness,
subtle profundity or profound subtlety, freedom from attachment, and tranquillity.

The Formless Self

Asymmetry. In contrast to paintings of Pure Land Buddhism that all show graceful figures that are perfect, symmetrical, well-rounded, and holy, Zen paintings negate these qualities. They are imperfect and worldly in the sense of going beyond ordinary perfection and holiness.

> Zen is a religion of non-holiness. Ordinarily, in religion, God or Buddha is something sacrosanct; in Zen, however, Buddha is non-holy as the negation and transcendence of holiness. Here also is the basis, in Zen art, of its *deformation*, which neither pursues nor is attached to perfection; it is of the nature, as Lin-chi said, of "killing the Buddha, killing the patriarch."[30]

Spinoza, who in some ways did not have much in common with Buddhism, nevertheless is very Buddhist in his understanding of perfection. He states that the most common way of speaking about perfection is analogous to the way men talk about good and evil. They have an ideal standard in mind, say of a house, and according to how something does nor does not measure up to this standard it is judged perfect or imperfect, good or evil. These are merely human ways of thinking and feeling; essentially they say nothing about the actual nature of what is being judged. Furthermore, such judgments make sense for Spinoza in a limited way only in relation to man-made objects, objects of *techne*; they are totally inapplicable and inappropriate to things of nature, which just are as they are and cannot be otherwise. Here Spinoza is close to the Buddhist theme of suchness (*tathata*).

Spinoza's own use of the word *perfection* (*perficere*) is closer to the nonjudgmental quality of being accomplished, completed, in this sense perfected. In keeping with his constant and vigorous rejection of final causes, Spinoza states that things are not put in the world by God to attain some end that they (and He) lack, but rather they endeavor to persist in and increase their being, coming as close to perfectedness as possible. But reality and perfection are the same thing.[31]

What Spinoza means by "perfection" is almost the dead opposite of what most people mean by perfection. It has nothing to do with "ideality." Rather, it has to do with the *isness* of things.

Simplicity. Simplicity is uncomplicated, uncluttered. It is not ornamental.

> If, as the negation of holiness results in the freedom of non-holiness, then simplicity as the negation of clutter may be spoken of as being "boundless" there is nothing limiting, as in a cloudless sky.[32]

We begin to see that the characteristics of Zen art are precisely those of absolute nothingness.

Austere Sublimity or Lofty Dryness. It makes little difference whether these words are being used as nouns or adjectives; they are functionally quite interchangeable. Thus, we could equally well say sublime austerity or dry loftiness. Two components are involved here: dryness or austerity and loftiness or sublimity. Dryness and austerity indicate a stage of life beyond sensuousness, fleshiness, immaturity, inexperience. It may mean a kind of "transcendental" beauty beyond the merely sensuous, as in painting, or a culminating fruition of practical wisdom, as in a Zen master. Sublimity or loftiness serves to intensify these qualities, indicating that they are not on a level accessible to just anyone and are attainable only after long practice.

Naturalness. This quality would seem to be self-explanatory, but it is not. It is not found in nature, in natural objects or in children. Again, like the preceding quality of lofty dryness, it is the culmination of long practice. It is well exemplified in Eugen Herrigel's book *Zen in the Art of Archery,* the first and best of the series of Zen in . . . to come. Herrigel had to learn to stop trying to shoot the arrow by improving his technique and just let "It" shoot. This took him six years. Such naturalness cannot be forced or constrained. It must be allowed to come about "of itself," and that is the root meaning of the term "spontaneous."

Subtle Profundity or Deep Reserve. This characteristic means that things are not explicitly spelled out in detail, but hint at an infinitude going far beyond, for example, the painted forms. Infinitude cannot be actually painted; it can only be hinted at, which in many ways is far more suggestive and powerful than any attempt at presenting it directly. Here, the viewer's imagination will far outstrip what is on paper. In addition, Hisamatsu addresses the qualities of darkness and massive stability. This darkness is calming, not ominous or threatening. By massive Hisamatsu does to mean mere heaviness, but the stability and unshakeability emanating from nonattachment, which leads to the next characteristic.

Freedom from Attachment. Freedom from attachment means not being bound by things, habit, or rules. People with many possessions are bound and fettered to these things: they take care of them, worry about their being lost, damaged or stolen, and insure them. But, of course, one cannot "insure" anything, least of all one's life. Freedom from attachment is perhaps better expressed by the word "unattachment" rather than the more common "detachment." Detachment can have the connotation that I simply don't care about a thing and want nothing to do with it. In unattachment, on the contrary, I can very well care about the thing— or person—and take care of it—or him or her—, but I am not bound by it. I can let go of it if that is what is called for. Hisamatsu places considerable emphasis on freedom from attachment as freedom from rules, custom, and ordinary logic.

Tranquility. Hisamatsu's examples are from the music in a Nō play and landscape paintings. The manifestation in sound or form is not disturbing, but rather induces calm, composure, and collectedness. The sound or form, so to speak, "gathers" the listener or viewer into itself.

Hisamatsu is careful to stress that these seven characteristics are all interrelated and are all to be found in any Zen art. Other art works of Buddhism or the West may possess one or two of them, but only Zen art invariably embodies them all.

In an effort to get beyond the reduction of "heart" to the physiological or the psychological, we brought in the neutral, mostly undeveloped term "mood." That led us into a discussion of Hisamatsu's seven characteristics of Zen culture. Now we need to focus back on just what he is talking about with these characteristics.

Hisamatsu is careful to emphasize that what is being expressed in the seven characteristics is not limited to art in the narrow sense, but extends to all spheres of human life. The Fundamental Subject of expression of the Zen fine arts is basically something that is beyond art.

What, then, is this Fundamental Subject? We are uncertain whether what is being discussed is what is being expressed or what is expressing itself. But, as was stated earlier, what is painting and what is being painted are the same.

Hisamatsu faces the question head on and states simply "Zen is the Self-Awareness of the Formless Self."[33]

Probing the meaning of formlessness, Hisamatsu asks the question whether there can be any mental activity that is beyond differentiation. Then he begins to show that what we ordinarily consider to be "mind" is already something objectified, thus possessing form. What the psychology, science, or philosophy of self-consciousness study is precisely not true self-consciousness, but an objectified self. And even when it is not so treated, self-consciousness, although it has no physical form, is still differentiated from all other self-consciousnesses, hence not truly formless. Thus, Zen formlessness does not coincide with the supposed formlessness of self-consciousness.

To further elucidate Zen formlessness, Hisamatsu refers to Dōgen's expression "body and mind fallen away." "Fallen away" is directly opposed to "transcend." We do not climb beyond or transcend the self, but body *and* mind drop off. It is not sufficient, as in some Western and Eastern philosophies, to transcend the body, the senses, emotions, and desires. There is nothing free or formless about our minds either. Formlessness means discarding the ordinary self, the self that has form and can still be differentiated.

Hisamatsu places considerable emphasis on the fact that he is not talking about the *idea* of a formless self, but about its existential *reality*.

> I think that nothing is more spiritual, nor anything purer than this Self. Further, in the ultimate or deepest meaning, when compared with this Self of Zen, everything else falls into the category of things—that which is objective. What is, will be, or has been objective are all things.[34]

The Self of Zen or the Formless Self cannot be defined or taught. We cannot look for it outside of ourselves or, for that matter, inside of ourselves either. For inside of ourselves is still differentiated from outside. In this sense, the Zen experience does not coincide with the "turning within" of Western philosophy which began with Plotinus and was followed by a few isolated thinkers.

The Zen experience of the Formless Self occurs only through what Hisamatsu calls "Awakening or *satori*."

> The attainment of *satori*, then, distinguishes Zen from ordinary religions. To attain *satori* is an activity quite different from intuiting, believing, knowing by intellect, or emotionally feeling, which usually obtain with ordinary religions.[35]

Taking up the statement from the Nirvana Sutra that "all sentient beings have the Buddha-nature, a statement that Dōgen amended to read "all sentient beings *are* the Buddha-nature, Hisamatsu explains that this should not be understood to mean that they are fundamentally Buddha but as yet have not realized this. That would constitute a distinction between the Original and the manifest.

Therefore, the ultimate or true meaning of the expression "every sentient being is originally Buddha" is that the Formless Self that I am—the Self of No-Form—is aware of itself. Since Self is synonymous with Self-Awareness, to say that the Self of No-Form is aware of itself is redundant. Accordingly, it is simply the Self of No-Form that is meant by the expression "every sentient being is originally Buddha."[36]

Buddhahood is not a matter of transcendence or immanence, but of *presence* or presencing. It does not inherently exist or presence in any particular time or space; if it did, it would be limited, not formless. It does not persist permanently in any time or space, but manifests itself instantaneously. Apart from this instantaneous manifestation, it "is" not. "Instantaneously" does not mean briefly. This manifestation cannot be measured. Rather, it indicates the sudden and abrupt nature of manifestation that ruptures all continuity of experience.

Now Hisamatsu delves into the *self* aspect of the Formless Self.

But the Formless Self is not only without form; it is *Self Without Form*. Since it is Self, its Formlessness is active; being without form, the Self is also active. Therefore Zen uses such terms as "rigidly void" and "merely void" for the kind of formless self that remains only formless. Again, when the self is never active and remains within formlessness, this is called "falling into the devil's cave."[37]

The Formless Self or absolute nothingness or Buddha not only is alive and self-aware; it is also constantly active. It appears through activity; what has no form takes on form. Only such form is true form. Whatever innately and essentially has form is bound and attached to that form; it is not free.

The form that constitutes the activity of the Formless Self, however, is the form of No-Form. For this kind of formless form, Zen has the term "wondrous being." This term signifies that, unlike ordinary being, this is at once being and nonbeing. Here, being never remains static, but is constantly one with Formlessness. So it is that the Formless Self is characterized as the True Void, and its appearance in form as "wondrous being"; and thus the Zen phrase, "True Void—Wondrous Being."[38]

This is Hisamatsu's interpretation of the Heart Sutra's "Form is nothing other than emptiness; emptiness is nothing other than form." Emptiness without form is rigid and merely void; form without emptiness is rigidly attached to form.

Hisamatsu discerns two aspects to *satori* or Awakening. First, the person gains freedom from what has form (body and mind drop off) and awakens to the Self without Form. Second, through its activity the Self without Form comes to assume form. Of course, "first" and "second" are makeshift terms here; there is no temporal sequence. There is only one and the same activity. After such Awakening, everything we see or hear or think is an expression of the Formless Self.

Since Hisamatsu finds that the Formless Self expressed itself in a certain period of Oriental culture, he now goes back to the seven characteristics he has discussed and inquires in what aspect of the Formless Self they are rooted.

Asymmetry. This is grounded in the negation of every form. Even a perfect form, and thus perfection in the ordinary sense, must be negated. Asymmetry is then the manifestation of No-Form as the negation of adherence to any perfection of form. Hisamatsu's examples for this are the preference for odd numbers over even ones, the crooked faces with lack of proportion of the arhats and the crooked and misshapen strokes in calligraphy.

Simplicity. Simplicity is also rooted in formlessness. The kind of simplicity Hisamatsu has in mind embraces both the simple and the complex. Thus, it is not to be confused with plainness. In addition, it negates color even when colors are present. It was Leibniz who stated that nothing is simpler than something.

Sublime Austerity. A basic feature of sublime austerity is that it is without sensuousness. But this does not mean that it is sheerly rational. Even reason is not completely free from the sensuous. It contrasts with it and is therefore related to and dependent upon sensuousness. Hisamatsu adduces the two words extremely central to Japanese aesthetic sensibility: *sabi*, being ancient and graceful, and *wabi*, having a poverty surpassing riches. These qualities are likewise beyond sensuousness, and thus beyond beauty as we ordinarily conceive it. As the adjective indicates we have here to do not with beauty, but with the sublime. It is beyond all weakness and insecurity. This sublimity is eons old, sturdy and seasoned. It embodies the dead opposite of the Western aesthetic ideals of youth and beauty.

Naturalness. Briefly, naturalness refers to the original manner of being before any artificiality or intent. This is sometimes indicated by the expression "No-Mind." It does not mean unconsciousness, but pure awareness without design or scheme.

Profound subtlety. The infinite depths of profound subtlety can never be fathomed or exhausted. Hisamatsu emphasizes its darkness that is filled with calm and peace. It is bottomless, generating endless reverberations going far beyond what was actually expressed. Yet without what was expressed we would have no inkling of its inexhaustibility and immeasurability.

Freedom from attachment. This characteristic of the Formless Self indicates that the Formless Self is ever free from form even while in the world. Thus, it is free to take on any form because of not inherently having any form. The actions of such a person embodying the Formless Self are carried out at lightning speed with unwavering immediacy. The opposite of this would be to be embroiled and entangled in the affairs of the world, which we mostly are. Heidegger would speak of inauthenticity, *Uneigentlichkeit*, the way we are "initially and for the most part."

Tranquility. Tranquility is related to the deep calm associated with profound subtlety. It is utterly free of disturbance and per-turbability. This means that nothing appears to any of the five senses and, above all, nothing is stirring in the mind. The mind or Formless Self is at rest even amidst motion and commotion. It was Heraclitus who said: "By changing it rests."

The characteristics belonging to the Formless Self discussed here constitute man's true and ultimate manner of being.

If one negates the customary meaning of mind as subject rep-resenting an object, one gets an immediate awareness that might provisionally be termed "seeing." If I "see" something without objectifying or even representing or picturing, what is actually happening?

The attempts to describe this kind of seeing or thinking are of necessity so repetitious that one begins to take them as platitudes. Nevertheless, they are platitudes that have never been under-stood. They are encountered on a purely verbal, logical level. They have never been penetrated.

The gist of these uncomprehended "platitudes" pretty much boils down to the phrase: an awareness that precedes or super-sedes the bifurcation of subject and object. We shall start with this and see if we cannot penetrate a little further.

In his most insightful book, *Toward a Philosophy of Zen Bud-dhism,* Toshihiko Izutsu distinguishes between consciousness of and consciousness pure and simple.

> Though similar in verbal form, "consciousness pure and simple" and "consciousness of" are worlds apart. For the former is an absolute, metaphysical awareness without the thinking subject and without the object thought of.[39]

Actually, seeing or even thinking might be a term preferable to consciousness since the latter is particularly strongly associated with "consciousness of," especially since Husserl. But it is pre-cisely the structure of consciousness of, of intentionality, that is to be eliminated here. Put in a vastly oversimplified fashion, for Husserl consciousness of or intentionality was meant to establish a link between consciousness and its intended object. It was meant to establish the directedness of consciousness toward a world outside of itself. But the schema outside-inside, outer-inner, the limitations of which Kant already pointed out in his amphibolies of reflection, have no place in the kind of seeing or thinking that we are trying to throw light on.

Not only thinking of, but also thinking *about* are inappropriate here. In that sense, seeing is perhaps the most appropriate term since we cannot even speak of seeing of or seeing about. Seeing is direct and immediate. But thinking, a special kind of thinking, can also be direct and immediate. And just as we do not mean by seeing simple, sensuous, empirical seeing, seeing and thinking are much closer to each other than is normally believed.

What is happening, what is at stake, at *play*, in this extraordinary use of seeing and thinking? To facilitate our understanding, let us take a look at the *Sansuikyō* (The Mountain-and-waters Sutra) fascicle of Dōgen's *Shōbōgenzō*. "It is not only when humans and gods see water that we should study this; also investigate the way in which water sees water."[40]

Initially, Dōgen is saying that water should not be viewed exclusively from a human or even from a divine perspective, which is usually tantamount to a glorified human one. For example, fish see water a certain way; it is their life element, they cannot live without it. A bird, say, a seagull searching for a fish, sees water in a different way. Seaweed would see water in still another way; it grows in water.

> The realm of ultimacy must also be of a thousand and myriad kinds. To further reflect upon the meaning of this point: Although water is manifold for various beings it would seem that there is no original water, nor is there universal water for all beings. . . . Water liberates itself through water. Accordingly, water is not earth, water, fire,

wind, space, or consciousness. Water is not blue, yellow, red, white, or black, water is not sight, sound, smell, taste, touch, or idea. And yet water is realized, of itself, as earth, water, fire, wind, space, and all the rest.[41]

The reference to the senses and various colors is self-explanatory. The first listing refers to the Buddhist conception of the six elements that constitute sentient beings. Dōgen is saying that water *is* not all these things, yet it is *realized as* them. Thus, water cannot be equated with any particular things or qualities, but it realizes itself as any and all of them. This water is not just the empirical water that we use and drink. It is more akin to Thales' water; it is, so to speak, "metaphysical" water. Ultimately, water is an articulation of the non-articulated.

Water-seeing-water" means for Dōgen "water" illuminating itself and disclosing itself as the primordial Non-Articulated. . . . Since, however, the "water" at this stage of spiritual experience is no longer seen as an object of sight by a seeing subject, whether human, heavenly, or otherwise, and since it is "water" itself that is seeing water, the ontological articulation of reality nullifies, as it were, its own act of articulation. The result is a seeming contradiction: the reality *is* and *is not* articulated into "water." Otherwise expressed, the reality articulates itself before the eyes of an enlightened man like a flash into "water" and then it goes back instantaneously into the original state of non-articulation.[42]

What is Non-Articulated (emptiness) articulates itself as "something" (form) for a sudden instant and then returns to its non-articulated state. What is difficult for the Western mind to accept is the fact that the Non-Articulated is only "there" in that sudden flash as form; otherwise the Non-Articulated "is" not. We are accustomed to thinking the Absolute as something *there*, statically persisting, which then manifests itself. But the manifestation of the Absolute in no way *negates* the Absolute. In contrast to this, the Non-Articulated is literally no thing, nothing, emptiness. Expressed another way, "the Undifferentiated *ex-ists* only through its own differentiation."[43] "For from the Zen point of view, what we have *provisionally* articulated as the 'non-articulated' can never subsist apart from the infinitely variegated forms of its own articulation."[44]

The preceding pages have been a somewhat clumsy attempt to describe what is happening when the Non-Articulated is articulated. We must now try to link this description to what we were saying about the seeing or thinking that lacks the structure of subject-object. The seeing or thinking in question here is not just the activity of the individual, empirical mind. Instead, we are dealing with Mind, Reality aware of itself. This mind is supersensible and superrational without, however, being destructive of either sensibility or rationality. On the contrary, sensibility and rationality are possible only because of Mind. It will not help us to say that Mind is "universal" as opposed to individual mind. For Mind is absolutely non-substantial; it is No-Mind. Yet, like the Non-Articulated, Mind can only function when it is at one with our empirical consciousness.

The Mind is something noumenal which functions only in the phenomenal.[45]

The Buddhist Absolute can only be absolute No-thingness.

"Critique of the 'Unconscious'"

The Non-Articulated of No-Mind is something that has begun to attract some attention on the part of some innovative schools of Western psychology and psychiatry. Their efforts to a large extent converge in an attempt to "deconstruct" previous theories of the unconscious. A prime target here is, of course, Freud, but also Jung who was far more open to Eastern and to religious and nontraditional thought in general. The basic tenet of these innovative psychologists and psychiatrists is that there is no such thing as The Unconscious; there are quite simply facets of awareness that go *unnoticed*. These facets are not hidden in some receptacle that is in principle unavailable to us. If we can defocus our selective attention, they are available.

> The holding on of ego is somewhat different. It is an active, but *intermittent* grasping. It is like the grasping action of the hand that makes a fist. If the fist remains clenched all the time, it would cease to be a hand, and would become a different kind of bodily organ. A fist by definition is the *action of clenching* the open hand. Just as a fist can only form out of the neutral basis of an open hand, the grasping of ego can only assert itself out of non-ego, out of a nongrasping awareness. Without this neutral nongrasping ground to arise from and return to, ego's activity could not occur. This neutral ground is what is known in Buddhism as *egolessness*, open nondual awareness, the *ground* against which the *figure* of ego's grasping stands out.[46]

One could argue that the figure-ground paradigm is perhaps somewhat less appropriate than the schema form-emptiness, since "figure" only makes sense when set *against* ground, but this is less important than pursuing the insights gained here.

> We continually have little glimpses of egolessness in the gaps and spaces between thoughts, the transitive moments of consciousness. Ego is being born and dying every moment, in that every moment is new and open to possibility. Ego-centered thoughts are continually arising out of a more open, neutral awareness which surrounds them and eludes their grasp. We continually have to let

go of what we have already thought, accomplished, known, experienced, become. A sense of panic underlies these births and deaths, which creates further grasping and clenching. Ego, in some sense, is the panic about egolessness, arising in reaction to the unconditioned openness that underlies every moment of consciousness.[47]

It should be noted that the term "transitive" used here stems from William James who used it in the sense of "transitional."

This description not only shows the nonsubstantiality of ego in that the ego's very foundation is a more open, neutral awareness, but also shows that the whole of ego's activity is *momentary.* This means that in a literal, radical sense ego is born and dies *at every moment.* Not only is ego completely non-substantial, but its impermanence is such that it is incessantly being born and dying. Impermanence does not simply mean that something exists for a limited duration of time, but that nothing subsists, persists at all. This fundamental fact opens the door to the two possibilities of freedom and of panic. In the words of R. D. Laing: "*We* are unconscious of our minds. Our minds are not unconscious."[48]

That is quite a striking statement. What is "unconscious" is precisely the conscious mind that blocks out or "brackets" a considerable portion of its awareness. This is quite natural, since our interest tends to focus on particular people, things, and situations. But at some point, we should be able to become aware that there are other possibilities.

It is important to note at the outset, however, that meditation can never be completely understood objectively, with the categories of the thinking mind, precisely because its nature is to transcend these categories. Meditation is not so much a particular kind of experience, but is rather *a way of seeing through* experience, always eluding any attempt to pin it down conceptually.[49]

Meditation is probably a term vastly misunderstood by those who do not practice it and perhaps even by some who do. Of course, there are many different forms of meditation. What is being stressed here and what interests us is the fact that meditation is not some kind of trance or mindless blankness and quietude. Rather, it is an activity of intense receptivity to openness.

This new approach to unconscious functioning is based on a notion of the organism as already relating to the world in global ways prior to the articulations of thinking mind. The sense of being encompassed by a wisdom greater than oneself, which may be ascribed to an "unconscious mind," comes from this dependence of focal intelligence on the wider, organismic process that is always operating beyond its range. Since we cannot pinpoint focally this organismic totality, we tend to deny its reality, or treat it as "other," separate from ourselves. But conscious and unconscious are not necessarily opposing tendencies, as depth psychology contends; rather, focal attention and holistic ground are complementary modes of organism/environment relationship. The organismic ground, moreover, is not truly unknowable in that it may be directly contacted in wider states of awareness.[50]

This is a paradigm for the relation of conscious to unconscious material similar to the one mentioned previously. We are dealing here with focal attention and a holistic ground which, however, is not a solid ground, but very much in flux.

In meditation, awareness of an open ground breaks through when one wears out the projects and distractions of thought and emotion. Then there is a sudden gap in the steam of thought, a flash of clarity and openness. It is neither particularly mystical or ecstatic, nor any kind of in-

troverted self-consciousness, but a direct participation in
an egoless awareness.

Ignorance in this perspective is the lack of recognition
of this nonpersonal awareness that surrounds the objects
of thought and feeling, and the treating of the latter as
solid, substantial realities. This ignoring seems to be an
activity that is constantly re-created from moment to moment.[51]

These psychologists and thinkers are not only attempting to
get beyond the subject-object dualism; above all, they wish to
reinterpret what has been regarded as the dualism of the conscious and unconscious mind. Basically, they regard the Unconscious as a hypostasization. Even Jung's Collective Unconscious,
which is far more compatible with Eastern thinking than is
Freud's Id, is rejected on the grounds that it still has the con-
scious-unconscious dualism and operates according to the model
of "inner and outer," which Kant had unmasked as one of the amphibolies of the concepts of reflection, along with identity and difference, agreement and opposition, matter and form.[52] For this
reason, in spite of a basic willingness to consider Eastern and
other alternative ways of thinking, Jung had a basic mistrust of
meditation as a process of withdrawing into introversion with the
possible resultant loss of being able to cope with the "outer"
world.

> The unconscious is typically seen as "other"—alien, un-
> knowable, even threatening. In this perspective medita-
> tion is conceived as potentially dangerous, in that it may
> subject the ego to "the disintegrating powers of the un-
> conscious." Such possible confusions led the Zen teacher
> Hisamatsu after a conversation with Jung, to distinguish
> the open ground of awareness from the depth psychology
> model of the unconscious. The "unconscious" of psycho-
> analysis is quite different from the "no-mind" of Zen. In

the "unconscious" are the a posteriori "personal unconscious" and the a priori "impersonal unconscious,"
namely the "collective unconscious." They are both un-
known to the ego. But the "No-Mind" of Zen is, on the
contrary, not only known, but it is most clearly known, as
it is called . . . "always clearly aware." More exactly, it is
clearly self-awakening to itself "without separation between the knower and the known." "No-Mind" is a state
of mind clearly aware.[53]

3

The Self-Overcoming of Nihilism

In his earlier work, *The Self-Overcoming of Nihilism*, Nishitani
states that, if nihilism is anything, it is first of all a problem of the
self.[1] From the outset he takes this problem up as an *existential*
matter; it is not to be dealt with as a problem of society in general
or as any sort of problem viewed from outside by an objective
and objectifying observer. This does not relegate the problem of
the self to some kind of idiosyncratic, personal or even pathological domain. If it but be recognized, it is common to all human
being now, but it cannot be "solved" sociologically.

> On the one hand, nihilism is a problem that transcends
> time and space and is rooted in the essence of human
> being, an existential problem in which the being of the
> self is revealed to the self itself as something groundless.
> On the other hand, it is a historical and social phenome-
> non, an object of the study of history. The phenomenon
> of nihilism shows that our historical life has lost its
> ground as objective spirit, that the value system which
> supports this life has broken down, and that the entirety
> of social and historical life has loosened itself from its
> foundations.[2]

The existential problem of the self, always potentially present for the individual, at times takes on a historical dimension and becomes the actuality of an epoch. For Nishitani, the problem of the self has actualized itself as the problem of nihilism at the end of the ancient period and the medieval period in the West, and in Japan in the mappō[3] thinking of the Kamakura period. Nishitani sees the reemergence of nihilism in the modern period in Europe above all with Nietzsche and Dostoevsky. This material has been discussed extensively in contemporary Western thought so that further consideration is not absolutely necessary here. What is significant for the purposes of this study is the fact that Nishitani sets the problem of the self squarely in the center of his inquiry, and indicates the self's ineluctable relation to nihilism and nothingness. His emphasis in this work is on the crisis this problem has assumed now historically both in the West and East. But his basic tenet is that this relation is always there when one penetrates it existentially on a "religious" level.

After a final reference in this work to Nietzsche's conception of the self as body, to my knowledge a unique evaluation of this idea, we shall turn to the more mature work, *Religion and Nothingness*. The majority of Western interpreters of Nietzsche revel in his rejection of reason, Platonism, and Christianity, and overlook the undeniably spiritual dimension of his thought. This Nishitani does not do.

> The so-called "I," what we normally take as the self, is merely a frame of interpretation added to this life process after the fact. The true self is the source of the life process itself, the true body of the will to power. It is what I have called "the self itself" or "the self as such," and not what is ordinarily called the "self." The so-called "I" is a tool of this greater self. This I take to be what Nietzsche means when he speaks of "body." Therefore, even if this standpoint of body is one of affirmation, it is not the kind of standpoint that can be adopted simply by abandoning

"spiritual" things—which in any event are not so easily abandoned—any more than it is easy to escape the conscious "I." The body in Nietzsche is the kind of self that is conceived from the side of an ultimate self-awakening beyond self-consciousness, or what I referred to previously as "Existence." The affirmation is on the same level as that of the religious believer who can affirm a God beyond death.[4]

Nishitani clearly distinguishes between the "I," what is normally called the self, and the true self. The "I" is a frame of interpretation that is added to experience, referring it back to a supposed subject. It construes itself as "within" and everything else as objects "without." Far from being something *added* to the life process the true self is the *source* of that life process. This self is conceived or experienced from an ultimate self-awakening that is beyond ordinary consciousness and self-consciousness. It cannot be conceptualized, imagined, or anticipated. The true self does not coincide with our customary idea of self at all.

Religion and Nothingness

In *Religion and Nothingness*, Nishitani pursues his fundamental question of the self by confronting the question of nihility. Nihility he defines as "that which renders meaningless the meaning of life."[5] It is precisely consciousness and self-consciousness that discover the threat of nihility underlying all existence. But consciousness then turns away from this threat and busily seeks to find satisfaction and fulfillment in its worldly pursuits. Its attempt is at best only partially successful. What consciousness must ultimately do is to *become* that nihility and, in so doing, break through the field of consciousness and self-consciousness.

Consciousness is the field of relationships between those entities characterized as self and things. That is, it is the field of *beings* at which the nihility that lies beneath the ground of being remains covered over. At this level, even the self in its very subjectivity is only *represented* self-consciously as self. It is put through a kind of objectivization so as to be grasped as a being. Only when the self breaks through the field of consciousness, the field of *beings*, and stands on the ground of nihility is it able to achieve a subjectivity that can in no way be objectivized. (16)

As long as we are preoccupied solely with *beings*, taking self and things solely as beings, we can do no more than represent beings. This was also Heidegger's insight. But, instead of pursuing the question of being as Heidegger did, Nishitani seeks to penetrate nihility itself. Heidegger was fascinated by the nothing (*das Nichts*), but it never became as absolutely central for him as it did for Nishitani. The nothing as the veil of being (*Schleier des Seins*) is a different "metaphor" from that of nihility underlying existence.

As long as we are on the field of beings, we can only represent and objectify, not only things, but above all the self. The subjectivity lying beyond the dualism of subject-object is lost. This subjectivity is existential in Kierkegaard's sense of that word; it is not Cartesian. The nihility lying beneath the self is obscured.

The only way to get out of the field of beings is to encounter and break through nihility. This leads one to encounter and become what Nishitani calls the "single Great Doubt." All the scattered, trivial doubts that we often entertain converge into a single Doubt, and that is all there is. We *become* ourselves the Great Doubt.

It is no longer a question of a self that doubts something on the field of consciousness, but rather a point at which the field of consciousness has been erased. . . . When we speak of a grief "deep enough to drown the world and oneself with it," or of a joy that "sets one's hands a-flutter and one's feet a-dancing," we have this same sense of single-mindedness or of *becoming* what one experiences. But it matters not whether we call it single-mindedness or *samādhi*—it is not to be interpreted as a mere psychological state. The "mind" of "single-mindedness" is not mind in any psychological sense. (19)

Nishitani distances this Great Doubt not only from any kind of Cartesian methodological doubt, but also from anything psychological at all. He is not talking about a state of mind, but about reality.

Through the Great Doubt the self is brought to experience the nihility or relative nothingness lying at its ground. For Nishitani this nihility is intrinsically present in the structure of self, but has now erupted full-blown in the West as the crisis of nihilism in which we now live.

Basically, Nishitani wants to get beyond consciousness and self-consciousness that are bound up with the structure of subject-object. That this does not constitute a descent into the psychological unconscious should be clear. He is not talking about any kind of mental state, but about reality. As long as we are dealing with consciousness or self-consciousness we can only represent, objectify and substantialize reality, that is, distort it.

In an effort to convey more concretely what he means by a self that is not to be equated with consciousness or self-consciousness, Nishitani speaks of subjectivity and *ecstasis*. The subjectivity he has in mind is not part of the duality of subject-object, but lies beyond this duality and, for that matter, any possible duality. It is not the subjectivity of the ego. How then, are we to think this subjectivity?

What is more, we seem to find in Eckhart a more penetrating view of the awareness of subjectivity in man. This can be seen in his reasoning that the awareness of subjectivity arises out of an absolute negation passing over into an absolute affirmation. The subjectivity of the uncreated *I am* appears in Eckhart only after passing through the complete negation of—or detachment (*Abgeschiedenheit*) from—the subjectivity of egoity. (65)

What Eckhart calls the uncreated *I am* is identical with the godhead beyond god, or absolute nothingness. Created in the image of god, human being shares this structure of negation yielding affirmation, or what Nishitani speaks of as a special kind of ecstasy. For Heidegger, ecstasy has the same etymology as the term existence, and means to step or stand out of oneself. This is a negation moving from self to the ground of self.

Ecstasy represents an orientation from self to the *ground* of self, from God to the *ground* of God—from being to nothingness. Negation-*sive*-affirmation represents an orientation from nothingness to being. (62)

Why is negation so crucial for Nishitani, and exactly what is being negated? What must be negated is the encapsulated self-reflection of the ego that would make the ego the center of everything. On an ethical plane this is quite easy to understand. As long as someone makes himself the center, it is impossible for him to get out of this confinement to achieve some "altruistic" act or attitude. Even if he did achieve an altruistic act, it would still be self-centered in that he would think, congratulating himself, *I* am altruistic and unselfish.

On a "structural" level, this is a bit more difficult to realize in Nishitani's double sense of realization as understanding and actualization. To realize one's dream means that the dream comes true, one becomes the dream. Tillich had something quite similar in mind when he interpreted "understand" as *standing under* the place of something, so to speak, as becoming its ground.

What must happen with negation on a structural level is that it must shift from the level of mere thought to that of existence.

Absolute nothingness, wherein even that "is" is negated, is not possible as a nothingness that is thought but only as a nothingness that is lived. It was remarked above that behind person there is nothing at all, that is, that "nothing at all" is what stands behind person. But this assertion does not come about as a conceptual conversion, but only as an existential conversion away from the mode of being person-centered person. (70)

Nishitani distinguishes here between the existential movements of ecstasy and of negation-*sive*-affirmation. Ecstasy is the movement of the self's stepping out of and over itself; it is thus a peculiar kind of "transcendence." "Where" it transcends to is nothingness, a *relative* nothingness. The subjectivity involved in this ecstasy already entails the death of ego and of consciousness as it is commonly understood. But ecstasy for Nishitani is incomplete; it does not go far enough. In order to be utterly free of person-centered self-prehension encapsulated and trapped within itself, what Nishitani calls "negation-*sive*-affirmation" is needed. On this standpoint, man is not man; he is a manifestation of absolute nothingness. But, as Nishitani repeatedly stresses, absolute nothingness is not a *thing* manifesting itself in and as man. Man does not manifest a *thing* called "absolute nothingness." He is an appearance with absolutely nothing behind it to make an appearance. Put somewhat differently, he is a form of non-Form. Or, to use Hisamatsu's phrase, he is a Formless Self. Ultimately, man is not man, is not human consciousness. With this, Nishitani has left all traces of anthropomorphism behind.

Granted what we have said about person-centered self-prehension of person as being intertwined with the very essence and realization of the personal, the negation of person-centeredness must amount to an existential self-negation of man as person. The shift of man as person to self-revelation as the manifestation of absolute nothingness . . . requires an existential conversion, a change of heart within man himself. (70)

Absolute nothingness becomes realized, actualized in a concrete human existence as a form of non-Form. Without the concrete form, absolute nothingness could not be manifested and actualized. Without absolute nothingness, the form could not be what it is. Absolute nothingness "is" only as the concrete form. Otherwise it is not at all.

In an attempt to get beyond the field of reason which always apprehends things substantively as *what* (*eidos*) they disclose themselves to us, Nishitani wants to attain access to things as they are apart from this disclosure. He wants to get at the "self-identity" of things, which does not coincide with their being conceived as substance or a "what."

> The true mode of being of a thing as it is in itself, its self-ness for itself, cannot, however, be a self-identity in the sense of such a substance. Indeed, this true mode must include a complete negation of such self-identity, and with it a conversion of the standpoint of reason and all logical thinking. (117)

The key to gaining access to something on its own home-ground lies in the negation of the self-identity apprehended by reason and *logos*. Nishitani's examples are: fire does not burn fire, water does not wet water, the eye does not see the eye. He appeals again and again to the well-known, absolutely central formula of the *Diamond Sutra:* A is not A, therefore it is A. The reason that fire can burn anything is that it does not burn itself.

> In contrast to the notion of substance which comprehends the selfness of fire in its fire-nature (and thus as *being*), the true selfness of fire lies its non-fire nature. The selfness of fire lies in non-combustion. Of course, this

non-combustion is not something apart from combustion: fire is non-combustive in its very act of combustion. It does not burn itself. (117)

The field beyond that of reason or *logos* is the field of emptiness (*śūnyatā*). For Nishitani, in order to arrive at the field of emptiness, the self must discover and experience its own nihility. It must realize that it is absolutely nonsubstantial. Nishitani states that such a transition from the field of nihility to the field of emptiness must take place, but does not go on to describe it in any detail.

The meaning of this turn to the field of *śūnyatā* has already been explained. Namely, when nihility opens up at the ground of the self itself, it is not only perceived simply as a nihility that seems to be outside of the self. It is drawn into the self itself by the subject that views the self as empty. It becomes the field of ecstatic transcendence of the subject, and from there turns once more to the standpoint of *śūnyatā* as the absolute near side where emptiness is self. (151)

Once again we have the elusive transition from ecstatic transcendence to the standpoint of *śūnyatā* or negation-*sive*-affirmation. Another way to state it is the transition from the self is empty (ecstatic transcendence) to emptiness is the self. The self's realization that it is empty is the necessary precondition for the stage of emptiness is the self to come about. Nishitani also calls this "true-self-awareness."

To be on such a home-ground of our own is, for us, true *self-awareness*. Of course, the self-awareness is not a self-consciousness or a self-knowledge, nor is it anything akin to intellectual intuition. We are used to seeing the self as something that knows itself. We think of the self as be-

coming conscious of itself, understanding itself, or intel-
lectually intuiting itself. But what is called here "self-
awareness" is in no sense the self's knowing of itself.
Quite to the contrary, it is the point at which such a "self"
and such "knowledge" are emptied. (152)

What Nishitani is asking us to do is subvert everything we
normally associate with self-awareness; it is not consciousness,
knowledge, or intuition, not even the intellectual intuition so
scorned by rationalist philosophers. The English word "awareness" obviates anything like a subject-object division, and it is
also etymologically related to the German word for "true," *wahr*.
It is in no way representational or objectifying. Nishitani's con-
tention is that what we usually think of as our "self" is actually a
representation of that self. He wants to arrive at some immediate
sense of self, even more immediate than intellectual intuition.
And since that self is in no sense any *thing*, the awareness comes
about as a merging of awareness with "world." After all, the field
of *śūnyatā* is a field of *force*. It cannot be represented or objectified.

If self-awareness is not the self's knowing of itself, what exactly is it? Nishitani returns again and again to the examples of
what might provisionally be called, for lack of a better term, "reflexive" negation. The condition of the possibility of the eye's
being able to see lies in the fact that it does not see itself. If the eye
saw itself, it could see nothing else. Other examples given are that
fire does not burn itself and water does not wet itself.

Similarly, whereas the ego sees and is concerned primarily
with itself, the true self sees not itself, but the "world," things of
nature, and other living beings. The true self's seeing of the world
constitutes its *becoming* that world. This is a point brought out
more strongly in Nishitani's study of Nishida. In an extended discussion of principle, Nishitani defines it as "an independent and
self-sustaining unifying power existing prior to mind and matter."[6] He then states that "this principle should not be restricted to
the confines of individual subjective consciousness. Anything so

grasped is," in Nishida's words, but "a footprint of principle at work and not principle itself. Principle itself is creative. We can *become* it and work in accord with it, but it is not something we can see as an object of consciousness."[7]

How can this experience of becoming something or becoming principle be elucidated? The Western thinker who perhaps best understood this phenomenon was Plotinus.

> One must therefore run up above knowledge and in no way depart from being one, but one must depart from knowledge and things known, and from every other, even beautiful, object of vision. For every beautiful thing is posterior to that One, and comes from it, as all the light of day comes from the sun. Therefore, Plato says, "it cannot be spoken or written, but we speak and write impelling towards it and wakening from reasonings to the vision of it, as if showing the way to someone who wants to have a view of something. For teaching goes as far as the road and the travelling, but the vision is the task of someone who has already resolved to see. . . . For that One is not absent from any, and absent from all, so that in its presence it is not present except to those who are able and prepared to receive it, so as to be in accord with it and as if grasp it and touch it in their likeness; and, by the power in oneself akin to that which comes from the One, when someone is as he was when he came from him, he is already able to see as it is the nature of that God to be seen.[8]

Whereas the "nature" of seeing in Plotinus is very close to what Nishida describes, "what" is seen is quite different. For Plotinus, this kind of seeing is only appropriate or even possible with regard to the One. Anything else seen remains on the "outside." For Nishida, this kind of seeing can relate to anything, a flower or a tree, for instance.

In this work, Nishitani retains the phrase "intellectual intuition" to denote Nishida's concept of "pure experience," a concept that shows the influence of William James. He also uses the
perhaps more appropriate phrase "empowering intuition" to
show that this intuition is nothing "passive." In *Religion and Nothingness,* he speaks of the field of emptiness as a field of force; thus,
again, nothingness is nothing passive.

Still pursuing what he calls "self-awareness," Nishitani states:

> This self-awareness, in contrast with what is usually
> taken as the self's knowing of itself, is not a "knowing"
> that consists in the self's turning to itself and refracting
> into itself. It is not a "reflective" knowing. What is more,
> the intuitive knowledge or intellectual intuition that are
> ordinarily set up in opposition to reflective knowledge
> leave in their wake a duality of seer and seen, and to that
> extent still show traces of "reflection." I call this self-
> awareness a knowing of non-knowing because it is a
> knowing that comes about not as a *refraction* of the self
> bent into the self but only on a position that is, as it were,
> absolutely straightforward or *protensive.*[9]

By "protensive" Nishitani does not mean that the self projects
itself in the sense used by Husserl or even Heidegger, but simply
that the "direction" in which the self moves is *away* from itself in
contrast to being reflected or refracted back into itself. The self
"stretches" forward, not back.

> This self-awareness is constituted only on the field of
> *śūnyatā,* on a standpoint where emptiness is self. The ab-
> solutely protensive position referred to is the point at
> which the self is truly the self in itself, and where the
> being of the self essentially posits itself. The knowing of
> non-knowing comes about only as the *realization* (mani-
> festation-*sive*-apprehension) of such being as it is in itself

on the field of *śūnyatā*. On all other fields the self is at all times reflective and, as we said before, caught in its own grasp in the act of grasping itself, and caught in the grasp of things in its attempt to grasp them.[10]

"In itself," of course, does not refer to a noumenon as opposed to a phenomenon, but simply refers to a thing as it really is undistorted by any interference with it. The term "realization" is important here. It denotes both our becoming aware of reality (I realize that *x* is true), and also "reality" (emptiness) realizing or actualizing itself in us. We become the "place" of realizing reality and reality's realizing itself. Nishitani also uses the term "appropriation" to further explicate what he means by "realization." In a footnote in *Nishida Kitarō*, we are told that the term appropriation is meant to render the German *Aneignung*. The Japanese word means literally "transformation into the self."[11] There might appear to be a contradiction between things being transformed into the self and the self's moving protensively toward things, but this probably stems from the subject-object structure of our normal thinking. Here the often-quoted passage from Dōgen's *Genjō-kōan* can help us.

> To practice and confirm all things by conveying one's self to them, is illusion: for all things to advance forward and practice and confirm the self, is enlightenment.[12]

For Dōgen, it is not the "direction" in which the self moves that is important, but how this relation of self and things occurs. Practicing and confirming all things by conveying one's self to them is a deliberate, intentional manipulation on the part of the ego. Allowing all things to advance forward and practice and confirm the self constitutes the true self's becoming all things. Things advancing toward the self is in no way synonymous with reflection; the self's advancing toward things is in no way synonymous with protention.

Actually, Nishitani refers to the relation between self and things as one of "circuminsessional interpenetration" or, one might simplify, reciprocal, or mutual interpenetration, indicating that his main concern is not that of "direction." This field of circuminsessional interpretation is the field of *śūnyatā* as a field of force. This field is opened up through the absolute negation of the self-centeredness of the ego.

All things coming forward to practice and confirm the self coincides with the dropping off of body-mind. It is not the case that the mind or soul gets free of its body that is its prison (Plato). The whole dimension of body-mind with which we anxiously equate ourselves must be cast off. Then the original face that we had before our parents were born can emerge. This is the place of what Nishitani calls "self-joyous *samādhi*" or "observance."

Hakuin (1685–1768), commenting on the occurrence of the word "observance" in the Heart Sutra, notes in effect:

> What about moving one's hands and feet, or eating and drinking? What about the moving of the clouds, the flowing of the rivers, the falling of the leaves, and the flowers scattering about in the wind? As soon as one tries to affix any Form to them, however slight, the result is bound to be the same as Chuang-tsu's fable about Chaos: gouging Chaos out and putting an eyeball there in its stead. Chaos dies.
>
> . . . We have no cause to inflict a wound on this Order by letting an act of reflective thought intervene, by fashioning an eyeball for it. No sooner has the attitude of objective representation come on the scene than "Form," as something outside the self, is generated; something that is not of one's own treasure house and not at one's own disposition shows up. Chaos dies.[13]

When we represent things objectively, as is our wont, we generate form as something external to us and fixate on that. But for

Nishitani, our moving our limbs, clouds floating in the sky, water flowing, leaves falling, and blossoms scattering are all ultimately non-Form. To adopt these forms of non-Form as the form of the self is precisely to *realize* (in the double sense) the Formless Self.

We need to address Nishitani's treatment of reality and illusion that does not coincide with any Western conceptions of that relation. In the chapter on "The Personal and the Impersonal," Nishitani states that person is an appearance with nothing at all behind it to make an appearance. How are we to think this kind of appearance?

The term appearance is essentially ambiguous. On the one hand, it can be equated with illusion. For example, He appeared to be healthy, but was in reality quite ill. On the other hand, appearance can indicate something real. For example, He appeared in the doorway. He put in an appearance at the meeting. In the first instance, appearance masks something that does not appear. In the second, no such duality is involved. Yet in a sense something can be said to be *behind* the appearance insofar as the person cannot be entirely equated with his appearance in the doorway or at the meeting. A principal distinction between the two instances lies in the lack of any element of illusion or deception in the second.

Nishitani's discussion of appearance lies closer to the second instance in that it involves no duality and no illusion in the sense that something behind it is being concealed. And yet it does involve some kind of illusion. Nishitani speaks here of "shadow" and "mask."

> Personality is something altogether alive. Even if we consider it to be "spirit," it is a mask of absolute nothingness precisely as *living* spirit. Were nothingness to be thought apart from its mask, it would become an idea. Were we to deal with the mask apart from nothingness, person could not avoid becoming self-centered. The living activity of person, in its very aliveness, is a manifestation of absolute nothingness. (72)

Nothingness cannot be realized (in the double sense) apart from its mask. If I think of nothingness by itself, apart from its mask, I am doing just that, thinking it *as an idea*. Nothingness can become an object of thought only as an object, as a *thing*. But nothingness is in no sense of the word a thing. Nothingness can only be realized existentially.

On the other hand, if we attempt to deal with the mask apart from nothingness, we are back in the self-centered, reflexive mode that we are trying to get away from.

> "Shadow" here means the same as what I called "illusion" above. It is the completely unreal, because all the activities of man become manifest as themselves only in unison with absolute nothingness. And yet precisely at this point they are seen to be the most real of realities because they are nothing other than the manifestation of absolute selfhood. (73)

Considered in unison with absolute selfhood, shadow is completely real; considered by itself apart from that selfhood, it is utterly illusory. Shadow and absolute nothingness cannot *exist* apart from each other.

Nishitani repeatedly stresses that, in order to view things in this manner, it is necessary to get beyond senses *and* reason, beyond consciousness, intellect, and our fixation on body-and-mind.

> Therefore, the elemental mode of being, as such, is illusory appearance. And things themselves, as such, are phenomena. Consequently, when we speak of illusory appearance, we do not mean that there are real beings in addition that merely happen to adopt illusory guises to appear in. Precisely because it is *appearance*, and not some*thing* that appears, this appearance is illusory at the elemental level in its very reality, and real in its very illu-

soriness. In my view, we can use the term the ancients used, "the middle," to denote this, since it is the term that seems to bring out the distinctive feature of the mode of being of things in themselves. (129)

Nishitani comes at the same fundamental thought again and again from different perspectives. "The middle" is a term he uses frequently in this book without much further clarification. Nor does he specify which ancients used it. What we have is "pure" appearance, and not some *thing* that appears. The middle might mean that there is no thing that appears on the one side, and no guise that it puts on on the other side. There is just the middle, as in the middle way between permanence (the thing) and nihilism (the guise). Nishitani also designates this situation as a thing as it is on its own home-ground, as it is in itself without any regard to our representations and judgments. Needless to say, the thing as it is in itself neither coincides with the Kantian noumenon, nor is it "unknowable." It can be experienced on the field of *śūnyatā*. Each and every thing as it is in itself is an absolute center.

To say that each thing is an absolute center means that wherever a thing *is*, the world *worlds*. And this, in turn, means that each thing, by being in its own home-ground, is in the home-ground of all beings; and, conversely, that in being in the home-ground of all, each is in its own home-ground. (As I have stated repeatedly, this relationship is inconceivable except in the nonobjective mode of being of things where they are what they are in themselves.) (164)

To repeat, the expression "things in themselves" means things as they really are, undistorted by the conceptual overlay that we impose on them. The closest Western analogue to this idea of each thing being in its home-ground while at the same time being in the home-ground of all other things—an idea having its roots in

Hua-yen Buddhism—is probably Leibniz's monads. Each monad is a world, containing everything implicitly within itself while mirroring all other monads.

> A thing is truly an illusory appearance at the precise point that it is truly a thing in itself.
>
> As the saying goes, "A bird flies and it is like a bird. A fish swims and it looks like a fish. The selfness of the flying bird in flight consists of its being *like* a bird. The selfness of the fish as it swims consists of looking *like* a fish. Or put the other way around, the "likeness" of the flying bird and the swimming fish is nothing other than their true "suchness." We spoke earlier of this mode of being in which a thing is on its own home-ground as a mode of being in the "middle" or in its own "position." We also referred to it as *samādhi*-being. (139)

This is strongly reminiscent of Dōgen's *juhōi*, the dharma-position or situation of a thing where it dwells.

In order to experience things as they are in themselves in the mode of being in the "middle," Nishitani explains that we need another Copernican revolution. Kant had shown that it is not we who must conform to things in order to know them (dogmatic metaphysics or sensuous realism), but things must conform to our faculties of sense and understanding. Now it is once again we who must conform to things. On the field of emptiness this means that we *become* the thing.

> The thing in itself becomes manifest at bottom in its own "middle" which can in no way ever be objectified. Non-objective knowledge of it, the knowing of non-knowing, means that we revert to the "middle" of the thing itself. It means that we straighten ourselves out by turning to what does not respond to our turning, orientating ourselves to what negates our every orientation. Even a sin-

gle stone or blade of grass demands as much from us. The
pine demands that we learn of the pine, the bamboo that
we learn of bamboo. By pulling away from our ordinary
self-centered mode of being (where, in our attempts to
grasp the self, we get caught in its grasp), and by taking
hold of things where things have a hold on themselves, so
do we revert to the "middle" of things themselves. (Of
course, this "middle" does not denote an "inside," as I
pointed out earlier on.) (140)

Earlier in the book Nishitani had already abolished the conceptual framework of "outside-inside," what Kant called one of
the amphibolies of reflection. The middle is not *inside* the thing; it
is the *center* of the thing. Ordinary knowing positions itself at the
circumference of the thing, thereby objectifying it. The kind of relation to the thing that Nishitani is talking about involves a mind of
non-discernment.

The mind we are speaking of here is the non-discerning
mind that is the absolute negation of the discernment of
consciousness or intellect. . . . In any case, the non-
discerning mind at issue here is not something subjective
in the manner of what is ordinarily called mind. It is a
field that lets the being of all things be, a field on which all
things can be themselves on their own home-grounds, the
field of *śūnyatā* that I have called the field of the elemental possibility of the existence of all things. (181–82)

The non-discerning mind does not single out, bifurcate or se-
lect. It lets things be as they are. This is the "mind" after body-
and-mind have dropped off.

Hence, when we say "mind" and "life" here, we mean
mind and life on the field where body-and-mind "drops
off," and where the "dropped off" body-and-mind is pre-

sent in full self-awareness and openness to the vitality of life. This "body-and-mind" does not refer simply to "thing" and "consciousness" in their ordinary senses. Nor is this body-and-mind on a field where it can become an object of study for physics, physiology, psychology, and the like. As Dōgen put it, "The dropping off of body-and-mind is neither form [thing] nor consciousness." (184)

We need to dispense with our ordinary idea of what body and mind are. This is enormously difficult to do. Western philosophers, ever since Plato, have pondered over the relation between body and mind, mostly with a detrimental assessment of the body. The fact that, since Nietzsche, the body has regained some measure of centrality does not alter much in this state of affairs.

Nishitani takes up the Western concept of the "natural light" and gives it a completely new twist. For him it is not the God-given light of human *reason*.

> This is why the "natural light" within us was spoken of earlier as the light of the things themselves coming to us from all things. The light that illumines us from our own home-ground and brings us back to an elemental self-awareness is but the nonobjective being of things as they are in themselves on the field where all things are manifest from their own home-ground. (164)

We receive our "natural light" not from God, but from things. It is not "inside" of us. It emanates from each thing as an absolute center.

> The field of *śūnyatā* is a field whose center is everywhere. It is the field in which each and every thing—as an absolute center, possessed of an absolutely unique individuality—becomes manifest as it is in itself. To say that each thing is an absolute center means that wherever a thing is,

the world *worlds*. And this, in turn, means that each thing, by being in its own home-ground is in the home-ground of all beings; and, conversely, that in being on the home-ground of all, each is in its own home-ground. (164)

Here we have moved from the field of reason, the field of traditional Western philosophy, to the field of nihility, the field of nihilism discovered, opened up and diagnosed by Nietzsche, to the field of *śūnyatā*. When things are at one with emptiness by relinquishing their substantial mode of being, they are in what Nishitani variously terms the middle mode of being, the nonobjective (nonobjectified) mode of being as they are in themselves, and *samādhi*-being. Nishitani distances this "middle" from the middle as it has been conceived on the field of reason as the Aristotelian mean or Hegelian mediation. Nishitani's middle is immediate, in his expression "at hand" and "underfoot." We are, so to speak, standing on it.

> We noted earlier that the "natural light" is not the light of reason but the light of all things. What is here called "spiritual light" does not mean the light of the "soul" or the "spirit" in the ordinary sense of those words. It is rather a "*samādhi* of the Storehouse of the "Great Light" out of which the light of all things (namely, the being itself of all things) is coming to birth; it belongs to the nature of every human being. When we say that our self in itself is the original and most elemental "middle," we are pointing to nothing other than just this. (167)

Nishitani gives an interpretation of *karma*, linking it to Eastern thought including Hinduism and to Western thought as well. His interpretation, however, does not make any sharp division between them. What interests him is the awareness of an infinite drive which is at once voluntary and compulsory. We can maintain our existence in time only by constantly doing something.

Even when we rest or do "nothing," it is only in order to resume doing something. We are driven both to do and not to do. While we choose what particular activity to pursue, we think we are free, and to an extent we are. But it is not a true freedom and certainly not a freedom from karma. For with each debt that we pay off, we incur a new one. We never get to the dimension of what Nishitani calls "our home-ground" which provides access to real freedom. Nishitani speaks of an infinite finitude, which is akin to Hegel's bad infinity. It is the inability to stop, to break free of the self-centeredness which constitutes the core of everything we do. It constitutes the self-encapsulation of the self, from which it is unable to break free. Actually, the self does not want to break free; it does not realize the necessity to do so. The self strives to affirm itself, and what could be more natural than self-affirmation?

In the West, this infinite drive took on the form of will. With the merging of philosophy with Judeo-Christianity, the will of God became decisive. Whereas the Greeks lacked any developed concept of the will, human being, created in the image of God, likewise possessed free will. Descartes stated that the cause of error or evil lay in the fact that man's will was infinite, whereas his understanding was finite. The concept of the will escalated through the seventeenth-century rationalists to German Idealism culminating in Schelling's statement that all primal being is will. With Schopenhauer and Nietzsche, the will became irrational and nonrational, that is, it deteriorated to an endless drive.

With the increasing secularization in the modern period, things became more and more human-centered. While the universe of the medieval human was God-centered, beginning with Descartes that universe becomes increasingly human-centered until with Marx, Nietzsche, Feuerbach, and Freud, it not only becomes human-centered in the sense of his autonomous reason, but no longer governed by the "rational." This is experienced as a great freedom, a great relief.

But is it? A look at the philosophy, literature and art of this time in general will tell us that things are not so simple. Powerful as some of the depictions of life are, they can be pretty bleak (for example, Beckett). But as the theologian Paul Tillich said in *The Courage To Be*, the fact that these artists can express their despair is an indication that they have in some measure transcended it.[14] There is undoubtedly some truth in this, but we must ask: Is this the only "transcendence" open to us, to give expression to despair?

It is with problems such as these that Nishitani is wrestling. Following Nietzsche, he recognized the contemporary situation of nihilism, "the uncanny guest at the door," faced it squarely and struggled to overcome it, I believe successfully. We must continue for a while longer to circle around these main "themes" of *samādhi*-being, in itself (*jitai*), middle and the logic of *soku hi* (is and is not).

> Although from Nietzsche's stance, we can say that our self is, in fact, "that," we cannot say that "that" in itself is, in fact, our self. In other words, although we can speak of a "self *that is not a self*," one cannot yet speak of a "*self* that is not a self."[15]

In the first position, speaking of a "self that is not a self," the focus is on the ego-self attempting to deny itself. But the focus is still on the ego-self. I can go around proclaiming that *I* am not-self, and many people do just that. But nothing has changed, except possibly a certain pride in the supposed fact that the self is nonself. The focus must shift to a "*self* that is not a self." Here one forgets what it is that has been so forcefully denied. As Dōgen said, "To study the self is to forget the self." To get stuck in the view that is preoccupied with what it is denying, is hopeless.

A quote from Masaō Abe condenses all of these problematic designations into one paragraph.

> He (Nishitani) designates the standpoint of emptiness as the place where the inseparability of life and death, being

and nothingness, is established; as the place where personality as reality manifests itself just as it is; as "the place
of absolute life-qua-death"; as "the absolutely transcendent this-side that is identical with the absolutely transcendent other-side; as the "in itself" (*jitai*) distinguished
from both substance (*jittai*) and subject (*shutai*); as the
place in which all things dispersed and dismantled in nihility are once again restored to being; as the place of
beification or *Ichtung;* as "the place of great affirmation";
as the place of power in which all things in their "being"
are absolutely unique while arising together collectively
as one. Further, the way of being of things in the place of
emptiness is designated as "*samādhi*-being" in that all
things exhibit an "in itself" way of being as if in *samādhi;*
as "middle" in that each thing is true being precisely as
provisional manifestation and provisional manifestation
precisely as true being; as "Position" in that all things are
self-establishing in their original position; as "circumin-
sessionally interpenetrating" in that all things stand in a
relationship in which they are simultaneously master and
attendant to each other; and also as "thus-thus" (*nyo-nyo*),
"phantom-like *qua* true suchness (*nyogen soku nyojitsu*)
and "primal fact" (*genponteki jijitsu*).[16]

If we can once again say something about some of these
themes, we shall pretty much have exhausted what we are capable of for now.

We must bear in mind that what is being avoided here is any
possible kind of objectification or representation. Thus, the terms
employed in this attempt sound strange and unfamiliar, and we
are initially at a loss to make sense of them. Let us take as our
first term the "middle," the relation of what is phantom-like and
true suchness. This is a reformulation of what we are accustomed
to call the relation of illusion and reality. We are accustomed to
conceive the reality of something and of its distortion. This is not

a simultaneous relation; rather, the thing appears now as phantom-like and unreal, now as true being. The thing's phantom-like and unreal character has no "value" for us, we want ideally to abolish it.

But this is all seen from the "outside," from our viewpoint. It does not get at the thing as it truly is in itself. Not only that. Far from being something that is to be abolished, without the phantom-like character of the thing it could not appear at all. In the language of the Diamond Sutra, form can appear whereas emptiness cannot. And yet there is no form without emptiness, no emptiness without form.

> Therefore, the elemental mode of being, as such, is illusory appearance. And things themselves, as such, are phenomena. Consequently, when we speak of illusory appearances we do not mean that there are real beings in addition that merely happen to adopt illusory guises to appear in. Precisely because it is *appearance*, and not some*thing* that appears, this appearance is illusory at the elemental level in its very reality, and real in its very illusoriness. In my view, we can use the term the ancients used, "the middle" to denote this, since it is a term that seems to bring out the distinctive feature of the mode of being of things in themselves.[17]

What we have here is a new interpretation of the relation between reality and appearance, and a highly paradoxical one at that. It is not the case that reality is "real" and appearance is illusory. Rather, because we have here to do not with some *thing* that appears but with *appearance*; appearance is illusory in its very reality and real in its very illusoriness. Reality and appearance are not two separate "things." They are inseparable. One might say that they are two aspects of the same "thing." No matter how we bend language here, it is not quite capable of exhaustively expressing what Nishitani has in mind.

This mode of being in the middle cannot be approached on the field of reason and sensation, but only on the field of *śūnyatā*. Thus, we do not get the *eidos*, the form or outward appearance of a thing viewed from the outside. Neither do we "identify" with it through intuition. Outside and inside are ruled out. If we are not encapsulated within ourselves, it makes no sense to speak this way.

> The things themselves reveal themselves to us only when we leap from the circumference to the center, into their very selfness. The *leap* represents the opening up within ourselves of the field of *śūnyatā* as the absolute near side which, as we pointed out earlier, is more to the near side than we ourselves are. The *center* represents the point at which the being of things is constituted in unison with emptiness, the point at which they establish themselves, affirm themselves, and assume a "position." And there, settled into their position, things are in their *samādhi*-being.[18]

What differentiates this kind of "viewing" from intuition? The fact that not only does the viewer not remain *where* he is; he doesn't remain *who* he is. When he takes this existential leap, the field of emptiness opens up in him as the absolute near side. Here we have a "transcendence" that does not go beyond, but, so to speak, back into ourselves. For we are not ordinarily that "near" to ourselves. Who can say that he is customarily "near," *present* to himself? But the point is that the leap transposes him into the place at which things assume a "position" and settle there. Thus, they are in their *samādhi*-being. Drawing on Nicholas of Cusa, Nishitani says that the center is everywhere and there is no circumference.

> Of course, it is not, however, the case that any one thing alone is the center. The field of *śūnyatā* is a field whose

center is everywhere. It is the field in which each and every thing—as an absolute center, possessed of an absolutely unique individuality—becomes manifest as it is in itself. To say that each thing is an absolute center means that wherever a thing is, the world *worlds*. And this, in turn, means that each thing, by being in its home-ground, is in the home-ground of all, each in its own home-ground. (As I have stated repeatedly, this relationship is inconceivable except in the nonobjective mode of being of things where they are what they are in themselves.)[19]

This is Nishitani's modern characterization of the Buddhist concept of codependent origination, the interdependence and nonobstruction of things. The closest Western analogue is Leibniz with his monads each mirroring each other. But the monads are self-contained "worldlets" whereas things in the Buddhist view actually *interpenetrate* each other. This is a whole complex issue in itself that we cannot and need not go into further here. The important point is that in this worlding the self-awareness of reality takes place. This means both our becoming aware of reality and reality realizing itself in our awareness.

To return to our main topic, the Formless Self is the expression most characteristic of Hisamatsu. The full formulation that he uses to designate the nature of human being is F.A.S. F. refers to the element of formlessness, A.S. indicates the wondrous activity of this Formless Self, A. being the standpoint of All humankind and S. referring to the suprahistorical origin of that activity. Thus, the three dimensions of Self, World, and History are fully taken into account. We shall discuss each of these aspects separately.

All humankind constitutes the "width" dimension of Hisamatsu's triad. This means that the formless self, which Hisamatsu also designates as Oriental Nothingness, is the most profound root source of human being. It is by no means restricted to the East, but is absolutely universal. Hisamatsu states that it is called "Oriental Nothingness" solely because it has not yet been fully awakened to in the West. Unlike D. T. Suzuki, Nishitani, and Ueda Shizuteru, Hisamatsu seldom refers to Meister Eckhart, possibly because the Christian, theistic language appeared strange to him. Be that as it may, nothingness has never been a central theme in the mainstream of the Western tradition. Heidegger may represent a move in that direction, but as long as he insisted on the term 'being,' it is difficult to see more than allusions to nothingness. Nothingness as the veil of being and man's being held out into nothingness are at best suggestive and open to the possibility of nothingness, but this is not really sufficient. In the end, it has been the East that has thus far cultivated a sensitivity to absolute nothingness. But if we consider the "characteristics" of absolute nothingness, which Hisamatsu discusses as aspects of the Formless Self expressed in Zen art, it can hardly be said to be anything "Oriental."

Hisamatsu again discusses the seven characteristics of absolute nothingness, this time formulating them in a negative way. Asymmetry becomes no rule. This means the negation of anything fixed and possessing form. Thus, the negation of form becomes a vehicle for the manifestation of no form. This is about as far away from classic Greek statues, which represent idealized perfection of form, as possible. The crooked faces of the arhats, a preference for odd over even numbers and the crooked characters in Zen calligraphy are all instances of the negation of order, rule, and perfection.

Simplicity becomes no complexity. Since color is something specific, the simplest color is no color. Even when colors are actually present, they are negated as colors. And when complexity of form is present, it is negated as complexity. A deep simplicity, not a simpleness, shines beyond color and complexity. Hisamatsu gives examples from architecture and painting, also citing various activities of Zen masters that instantiate simplicity.

Sublime Austerity becomes no rank. This, of course, should remind us of the true man without rank or the uncarved block of Taoism. One might think that the expression "uncarved block" means a person of no education or refinement, someone untutored and uncultivated. But this is not at all what is meant. Neither does it mean exactly something like pristine. Rather, it is a negation of the sensuous and, insofar as reason is contrasted with the sensuous and thus to some extent dependent upon it, of reason also. Seasoned and sturdy, it is beyond beauty. It is sublime, a word of which we scarcely in this age can make any sense.

Naturalness becomes No-Mind. It might seem confusing when Buddhism says everything is Mind, and then turns around and speaks of No-Mind. It all depends on what is meant by mind. The mind that is negated in No-Mind is the "monkey mind," the mind filled with thoughts of this and that, thoughts which for the most part have nothing to do with anything. The incessant chatter going on in our heads has nothing to do with Mind. A good image for Mind is the mirror with nothing in it; it is thus capable of reflecting whatever comes before it. Clear and uncluttered, it simply gives back whatever comes to meet it.

Hisamatsu uses the term *sabi*, being ancient and graceful, to further characterize the quality of No-Mind. It is neither a naive naturalness nor a contrived artificiality. It is not a quality that we begin with, but something acquired. It is something so thoroughly acquired that we embody it, we become it and do not need to consciously think about how to do something. Artists and athletes to some extent necessarily have this quality. A dancer cannot constantly think about his footwork. Neither can a basketball player. We shall return to the question of No-Mind later which is so essential to understanding the Formless Self.

Subtle profundity or deep reserve becomes no bottom. This derives from the fact that no form can exhaustively express the formless. It can at best intimate that which cannot be expressed. Hisamatsu repeatedly uses the term reverberations to describe the intimation of the formless. When we listen to a sound, we follow it as it dies away. It never stops, but gradually disappears. Thus, no definite limit is set to our following and we enter another realm, that of the formless. We need not restrict these reverberations to the realm of hearing, however. A solitary bird or single boat can produce a similar effect.

Darkness also characterizes the quality of having no bottom. The darkness of the tearoom, for example, is not threatening, but contains an atmosphere of composure and calm. Much about the room is sensed, not exposed to any sort of glaring light.

Freedom from attachment becomes no hindrance. Nonattachment is not the same as detachment. Detachment from something means having nothing to do with it. The activity of the Formless Self, however, in expressing itself in the many forms of the world, is bound to none of them. The Formless Self must express itself concretely in shaping historical and artistic reality, but it never coincides with any one particular thing.

> But the formless self is not only without form; it is *Self* without form. Since it is Self, its formlessness is active; being without form, the Self is also active. Therefore Zen uses such terms as "rigidly void" and "merely void" for the kind of formless self that remains only formless. Again, when the self is never active and remains within formlessness, this is called "falling into the devil's cave."[20]

This represents the very antithesis of the bodhisattva ideal, attaining some kind of awakening or enlightenment and regarding this as a final goal. Apart from the question of just what this would look like, one awakens to something very alive and dynamic that enormously activates one and sends one straight back to the world. This is the meaning of compassion, *karuna*, apart from which *prajna*, transcendental insight, is useless. It is not even a matter of being "altruistic"; one just does what is to be done.

Freedom from attachment means that the Formless Self, while entering all the concrete forms and acting there, never gets stuck anywhere.

Finally, tranquillity becomes no stirring. This does not mean a static, lifeless state. It is rather rest within motion. When there is no distraction on the part of the senses and when the mind is not agitated, one is tranquil in one's activity. One acquires a steadiness that is unshakeable, imperturbable. Bashó's haiku about the frog jumping into the pond might serve as an example. There was complete stillness before the frog jumped. But his jumping does not disturb the stillness; rather, it only points it up, offsets and heightens it. After the plop has subsided, we really hear absolute stillness.

Hisamatsu is careful to point out that all of these seven characteristics are present in a Zen art work or in everyday activity. They are so close to each other as to be inseparable. They characterize the expression of the Formless Self, its taking on form and working therein. Otherwise we would remain at the eighth stage of the ox-herding pictures, the empty circle. We must go on to the ninth stage showing an old man and a younger one meeting along a roadside. Ueda Shizuteru gives an interesting interpretation of the last three stages, eight, nine, and ten, as being no longer, as in the preceding stages, a matter of gradual progression, but a kind of oscillating back and forth. The direction is reversible, meaning that one can move freely between nothingness, nature, and human communication.

> This same thing, the selfless self, is for its part only fully real insofar as it is able to realize itself in a totally different way in each aspect of this three-fold transformation: as absolute nothingness, as the simplicity of nature, and as the double self of communication. The final three stages portray as it were the three-in-one character of the true self. This means that the self is never "there" but always in the process of transformation, always fitted to its circumstances and likewise always proceeding from out of itself, at one moment passing away into nothingness unhindered and without a trace, at another, blooming in the flowers as the selfless self, and at a third, in the encounter with the other, converting that very encounter into its own self.[21]

The key sentence here is the self is never "there." It never persists statically throughout change. Thus the prime characteristic of the Western conception of self, its continuity of consciousness and self-identity, is conspicuously absent. We shall return to this point in a discussion of the length dimension, living the life of history while transcending history, the suprahistorical living of history.

But first we shall discuss the depth dimension. Of course, these three "aspects" of the Formless Self are hardly separable except for purposes of analysis. There remains of necessity a certain artificiality in discussing them in isolation. As stated before, we have to some extent already discussed this dimension in our discussion of the dimension of width.

The whole Kyoto school takes religion extremely seriously. Hisamatsu asks where in man is the "moment" which prevents man from remaining merely man? Put in a different way, where in man is the "moment" whereby he needs religion? "Moment" is being used in the Hegelian sense of a crucial factor. Hisamatsu is seeking a standpoint which is neither a theistic heteronomy nor rational autonomy. In other words, he is seeking a standpoint which is absolutely autonomous but not based solely on reason, although it includes the rational. The medieval type religions based on theonomy have been replaced by the humanism of autonomous reason. While affirming the element of autonomy, Hisamatsu sees in the "moment" in man which prevents him from remaining merely man the necessity to get beyond rational humanism.

What is this "moment?" It is to be found in the ultimate antinomy lying at the basis of the self. Hisamatsu interprets this ultimate antinomy in terms of sin and death, whereby "sin" must be taken in a qualified sense since it has not always been considered central in Buddhism. When Sakyamuni escaped his father's palace, what he encountered and what became the "moment" for his religious quest was not release from sin, but from sickness, old age, and death. Nevertheless, we want to see how Hisamatsu interprets sin, since he includes it in his discussion.

When we speak of original sin, which aspect do we point to? No mere dogma or doctrine or words—arrogant as it might sound to speak thus—attributed either to Sakyamuni or Jesus Christ or anyone else, would ever convince me that I have committed original sin. In this very respect one might well insist that I have *karma* accumulated from previously lives or that I have the stains of original sin on my soul. However, I have never been ashamed or worried that I might have such *karma*-accumulation or effects of original sin. I rather think that because I am affected thus the real situation of man becomes apparent and, far from feeling penitent, I take delight in it.[22]

The reason Hisamatsu takes delight in this ultimate antinomy is that, by being aware of it, the possibility is afforded of extricating oneself from it. To take relative antinomies in the moral sphere is to remain blind to the ultimate antinomy and thus to be stuck in it. Sin for him extends beyond morality to the sphere of science and art as well. It is evident in the antinomies of evil versus good, falsity versus truth, ugliness versus beauty and defilement versus purity. This he calls the "abyss of man," the deep chasm from which he cannot escape. Most often relative reasons are given too much emphasis for situations such as the number of suicides or general nihilism, a problem which Nishitani also squarely faced and dealt with. One must grasp the ultimate antinomy lying at the root of human being.

Hisamatsu next takes up the question of death. Since for him death is inseparable from life, the problem is not to be found in death alone, but in the nature of life-and-death (*samsara*). He then deepens the antinomy of life-and death to the dimension of origination-and-extinction, which includes beings other than humans. Finally, he further deepens the dimension of origination-and-extinction to that of existence-and-nonexistence or being-and nonbeing. This ultimate antinomy of life-and-death or existence-and-nonexistence is ultimate death or, in Zen, the Great Death. This must not remain a mere concept; it must be realized *existentially*.

It might be said tentatively that what "precedes" the Great Death is the Great Doubt or doubting-mass, although, strictly speaking, there is no continuity of temporal sequence here, rather a complete turn-about *(pravrtti)* and shattering of what went before.

One reason there is such a break in continuity is that the way of being of the Formless Self comes breaking through the bottom of ultimate antinomy.

> By the seeing of one's Nature we do not mean any objective contemplation, objective awareness, or objective cognition of self-Nature or Buddha-Nature; we mean the awakening *of* the Self-Nature itself.[23]

The genitive is a *subjective* one. We do not awaken to self-nature as an object; rather, self-nature or Buddha-nature or the Formless Self itself awakens.

Hisamatsu stresses the fact that awakening is no extraordinary state, although it is unfortunately not very common, but the original way of being for us human beings. It is a way of being, not merely a state of consciousness or a special feeling.

Thus, the Formless Self is neither transcendent in the sense that it is outside of us and possibly attainable at some future time, nor is it immanent in the sense that it is simply "there." It is never "there," which is perhaps the most difficult thing for westerners to understand. If we say that it is "dynamic," to use this shopworn word for which we have no real fresher alternative, we mean that the Formless Self is the constantly awakening ultimate present.

Hisamatsu broaches the subject of how such an awakening is possible. Again taking up the subject of the ultimate antinomy that forms the very basis of reason, he finds it to have the two aspects of value-antivalue and existence-nonexistence. Herein lies

the ultimate source of all our worries and anxieties. This antinomy is insoluble. It is insoluble because what we want is pure,
eternal life, and this is impossible. It is impossible because life as
we know and live it is fundamentally life-death. When Buddhism
states that we are living and dying at every moment, this is no
mere metaphor. Our lives are shot through with loss, disappoint-
ment, failure, and the like. Of course, we also experience gain, fulfillment, and success. But they are fundamentally temporary.
Nothing lasts. Nothing is achieved once and for all. This is not a
cause for regret or despair. It is simple impermanence, the impermanence that we are.

But that is not all. This is going on *at every moment*. My consciousness is not, so to speak, a steady stream of thoughts and
feelings, as the expression "stream of consciousness" would indicate. It arises and perishes every instant. Otherwise, how could
one explain the occurrence of a new idea or of any kind of cre-
ativity. The language that the Kyoto school constantly uses to describe our root source is that of *bottomlessness*. Out of this
bottomlessness our awareness arises and perishes at every instant. We shall return to this rather fascinating question later.

It is in terms of this ultimate antinomy that the concept of
original sin is to be understood. The "sin" lies in the ultimate antinomy that forms the basis of reason. This is not our fault, nor is
anyone else responsible. It is simply the way things are. Thus,
original sin is not a moral question, but an ontological one.

How do we get free of this antinomy? Since the ultimate antinomy forms the basis of reason, we as rational beings cannot
solve it. The solution of most religions, Christianity and Shin
Buddhism, for example, lies in the hope of a future redemption
by another being, be it Christ or Amida Buddha. Hisamatsu
firmly rejects this point of view.

In any case, however, such religion's time never coincides
with historical time; religion of this kind is isolated and is
an escape from the actualities of life. For example if be-

coming a Buddha or having rebirth in the Pure Land is a
matter of a future life, since it occurs after the actual time
in which we live is completely terminated, that is, in the
future after death, then to attain it would be absolutely
impossible.[24]

This involves the question of the length dimension, the
Suprahistorical, to which we shall turn presently.

To recapitulate, neither I as a rational being nor anyone or
anything other than I can free me. It goes without saying that this
is also not to be accomplished by some irrational factor in me.
There is something in me that has nothing to do with rationality
or irrationality. That is the Formless Self. But unless we realize the
ultimate antinomy that is reason, there is no "moment" enabling
such a breakthrough. That is why Hisamatsu could say he took
delight in being affected by the real situation of man. The ultimate
antinomy offers him the most crucial and irreplaceable moment
to break free.

But it is only the moment, the occasion, the *kairos*, the catalyst.
Of itself the ultimately antinomic self cannot overcome the antinomy since that is, so to speak, what it is. Rather, the Formless Self
emerges from within the antinomy, it awakens. And this, again, is
nothing extraordinary: it is the true mode of man's being. We
said, and Hisamatsu said, there was a leap, a gap in continuity
here. But now he qualifies this further.

> Therefore, concerning the relation between the saved-self
> and the not-yet-saved-self, it is too delicate a matter to
> speak of either continuity or discontinuity.[25]

In spite of this statement, Hisamatsu does not pursue the
matter further. Rational autonomy becomes depth autonomy. I
believe the reason Hisamatsu says that the matter is too delicate
to be described as continuous or discontinuous lies in his concern
that we not take the awakened self as something separate from

ourselves which "saves" us. After all, we are normally "saved" by someone else, a savior or an Amida Buddha; we cannot save ourselves.

> Thus do positiveness and affirmativeness arise. That direction, which is the opposite of the one toward the original Self, brings about a positive continuity with it. Previously there was the self-negating continuity from the unawakened self to the awakened self. Now, on the contrary, there is effected the *affirmative, positive continuity from the awakened self to the unawakened self.* That comes to mean *resurrection or resuscitation of the self.* It is only here that one can speak of absolute affirmation.[26]

Negation takes place in the movement from the unawakened self to the Formless Self. What must be negated is the self based on reason and the senses. Affirmation, however, takes place when the rational self is resuscitated with the Formless Self as its source. The fact that it is resuscitated or resurrected means that some kind of death has taken place here, the death of the rational self. When it reemerges from the Formless Self it freely lives the rational life while transcending reason.

We turn now to the length dimension, that of the Suprahistorical. Hisamatsu uses this word in a different sense, say, from Nietzsche, for whom it meant that which is above time and timeless. For Hisamatsu, on the contrary, it is the *source* of time and space, that out of which they come. Hence it is in no way a negation of time and space, nor can it simply be equated with them.

> In other words, the world which had the rational self as its fundamental subject is converted to the world which has the awakened self as the fundamental subject. That world is not differently located in time and space from the ordinary world. Rather, it is the fountainhead of time and

space, in which time-and-space is established and from which time-and-space arises.[27]

Hisamatsu refers to the Suprahistorical also as "religious time." The traditional view of religious time he views as of a completely different order from historical time, intersecting historical time. One thinks of the *nunc stans*, the standing now lifted out of time. This is not the kind of eternal now that Hisamatsu means.

> The Buddha-nature is neither transcendent nor, in the ordinary sense, actual. It is the *constantly awakening ultimate present*. The awakened is the true Buddha-nature; the immanent is not yet the true Buddha-nature. Therefore, redemption points, more than anything else, to the presence of the saved. It is not a matter of either the future or the past. *One's being saved at the present time is the true way of redemption.*[28]

Although the language is to some extent Christian (redemption, being saved), the thought is distinctly Buddhist. Notice that where one would expect Hisamatsu to say the Buddha-nature is neither transcendent nor immanent, this is not what he says, although he denies immanence two sentences later. We know by now that it is not transcendent in the sense that it is beyond and outside of man. That it is not actual means that it has not become actualized as the result of a process leading from potentiality to actuality. It also means that it is not to be found there. Instead, it is *constantly awakening*. It is, so to speak, realized in an instant, and then gone. In an instant does not refer to any specific length of time, but to the suddenness of awakening. And then the Buddha-nature is gone, only to awaken again. It never "stays around." Neither is it immanent. This would again span it into the scheme of potentiality-actuality. The continuous substratum for such a process is lacking. As Dōgen said, we do not say that spring becomes summer. When it is spring, it is spring. When it is summer, it is summer. Spring is spring and summer is summer. One does not turn into the other. There is no transition.

This is particularly evident in the ordinary event of traveling somewhere. One is in one place and, particularly in the days of air travel, one is suddenly inexplicably in another. But even if the so-called transition is slower, say, by boat, one was still in one place and then one is in another. There is no transition.

> Religious time ought necessarily to be what coincides with historical time. I do not think that religious time is established in its relation to historical time by crossing the latter. I rather think that historical time is established with religious time as its fundamental subject.[29]

Religious time does not have to "cross" historical time because it is not "above" or outside of it. Rather, it is at the basis of history, creating history, but not bound by history. It is always freed from creation while constantly creating. Hisamatsu sums up the matter as follows.

> Only bringing an individual to the Formless Self, as has usually been the case with Zen, cannot be said to be the full, wondrous activity of the Formless Self. Leading an individual to the Formless Self to have him awake alone would leave him in the end with a Formless Self beyond which he could not go. The great activity of the Formless Self ought to work three-dimensionally so that it will not only lead the individual to the Formless Self but truly form the world and create history. Only then will its wondrous activity become full and its great Zen activity become world-forming and history-creating. That is to say, its Zen activity will have the three dimensions, Self, World, and History, which constitute the basic structure of man, closely united within itself. [30]

In a remarkable article with the unassuming title "Ordinary Mind," Hisamatsu pursues the question of Suprahistorical history in a seemingly indirect way. He begins by pointing out the contradictory elements in ordinary things of constancy and change or being and nonbeing. This contradiction eventually results in a synthesis which again affords man a sense of security and ease. But he must not mistake this aspect of synthesis of ordinary things for something permanent or eternal.

> That man views the world solely in its aspect of "being" or "nonbeing" is because he erroneously takes the synthetic aspect of ordinary things for something ultimate, or at least for something enduring. In other words, since man assumes anything that "is" to be ultimate in its existence, in health he forgets disease, in life he forgets death, in peace he forgets war, in order he forgets disorder.[31]

However, an ordinary thing is no mere synthesis. It contains at the same time an antithesis within itself, as it does in Hegel. But, as we shall presently see, Hegel's dialectic is quite different from that of Hisamatsu.

When only the aspect of antithesis or negation is perceived, one tends to fall into a pessimism which laments the transiency of life. This is as misguided as the opposite view of taking the synthesis achieved in things for something permanent or eternal. The absolutely cardinal principal of Buddhism applies here of the Middle Way, the strict avoidance of the extremes of externalism and nihilism. The Buddha discovered this ethically and existentially when he came to reject the luxury and comfort of his life in his father's palace (*eternalism*) and also found that extreme asceticism (*nihilism*) wasn't the solution either since it led ultimately only to death. He then deepened his understanding to the ontological level, perceiving the utterly false, hopelessly ingrained tendency to take all things as either eternal or permanent, or nihilistic. They are both, and this forms the contradiction at the heart of all things.

> If ordinary things were merely "being" (*u*), the movement of history would not materialize, while if they were merely "non-being" *(mu)*, the presentness of history would not make itself manifest. It is for this reason that the historical world is said to be being which is none other than non-being, non-being which is none other than being.[32]

Hisamatsu is critical of scholars of ethics, philosophy, and religion who approach their subject in an objective way, failing to incorporate it existentially in their lives. That this is indeed the case is the understatement of the year, if not the century. Hisamatsu then attempts to describe a kind of knowledge which is no mere objective knowledge, but is fundamentally subjective or existential and includes working or acting as an indispensable ingredient. This sort of existential knowledge he finds best instantiated by the masters and experts of the various Eastern arts and martial arts, although by no means necessarily limited to these.

> It is thus, having become the art-itself, that they may be called "incarnations" of their arts. This kind of "knowing" is different from the scientific Knowledge that is spoken of today, resembling, rather, what is called *"kotsu"* (knack, lit., bone, or pith) in Japanese. It is said to be something which is suddenly attained and self-acquired; it is not something that can be taught. (7)

However, here Hisamatsu is also critical, although to a much lesser extent. Outside of his art, such a person may encounter unanticipated barriers. One must become an accomplished master in the total matter of human existence. Applied to philosophy, this constitutes man's attempt to live in an ultimate manner.

> In other words, the total being *is* itself the task. That the total being, which is the task, elucidates itself in a total manner by means of itself, is to *live* philosophy. (12)

To live philosophy in this sense means to overcome the total contradiction of life in a total manner. Now we begin to see what is meant by the title of the essay "Ordinary Mind." The person who has resolved the contradiction not merely in a special field or art, but in his very life is considered a person of attainment. It is only in this kind of person of attainment that the true ordinary mind is to be found.

When the Zen master Nan-ch'uan was asked by a disciple, "What is the Way?" He responded, "Ordinary Mind is the Way." Hisamatsu elaborates on this in a lengthy footnote.

> The Zen Master Ma-tsu Tao-i used the term *heijōshin* [ordinary mind] in its original sense in which it is contrasted with *shojishin* (Life-and-death mind). . . . With both Matsu and Nan-ch'uan, *heijoshin* means the Ordinary Mind awakened to its true Self and functioning in its everyday activities—that is, what the author calls the creation of Suprahistorical history. (18)

What follows is a discussion of matter and form which we need not go into in its entirety here. Form as conceived by Plato was something transcendent which was already as "real" as it was ever going to be. There is no positive reason for form to combine with matter, to become "historical." Matter only serves to distort the Forms. For Aristotle and Plato form realizes itself through matter. But Hisamatsu rejects even this conception of form which is immanent and developing. It is not subjective or existential enough to be the "subject" of history. The term "subjective" here lies closest to Kierkegaard's understanding of that term, not as solipsistic or epistemologically isolated, but as what I am, what the self is. Anything not subjective in this sense lies in the domain of what is outside of me, of what can be objectified.

We want to take a closer look at this use of form which is, to say the least, rather peculiar. But set against the background of Hisamatsu's thought in general, it is, after all, comprehensible.

> The actualization of "form" is always self-limiting and finite. Form is experienced only in its self-limitation. It is said that form is only actualized as that which is actual in history. And yet it is thought that while form, through its actualization in history, limits itself and becomes finite, at the same time it transcends actuality and, being infinite, cuts off limitation. Only when form is taken in this sense can it be the form which is the subject of history. (20)

What Hisamatsu appears to mean by form is form actualizing itself in matter. Form actualizes itself through its self-limitation in matter. But it must again negate that limited self. Thus, Hisamatsu can equate this unusual meaning of form with absolute nothingness. Actually, he seems to see matter as equivalent to being.

> Furthermore, this subject of history, in that it eternally creates that which is historically actual, is "absolute being" and of immanent character, but at the same time, in that it eternally negates its self-limitation, it is "absolute nothingness" and of external and transcendent character. In this, form and matter are not dualistic. The self-limiting aspect of the subject which lives in history is matter; the negating aspect of self-limitation is form. (22)

Hisamatsu is aware that he is using form in a sense opposed to the predominant thinking of the Greeks, but he feels that the

Greeks saw only the self-limiting aspect of form and overlooked the negating aspect of self-limitation. However that may be, it is clear that he wants to see a positive and creative meaning in history which was predominantly lacking in the Greeks. But history for him, while possessing a positive meaning, cannot be self-supporting or be all that there is. His own standpoint after all, is that of religion, and the fact that man has religion is evidence that he can never be satisfied with the view that history is everything.

> To live in history without being aware of the abyss of this ultimate contradiction, which lies at the foundation of history itself, is just as if one were to hold a thousand-ton bomb and stare down into a ten-thousand-foot pit. . . . This explains why contradiction is irresolvable within the historical dialectic, and it even explains the necessity of advancing to what may be called the "religious dialectic." (26)

Herein lies the Suprahistorical task of the Formless Self. The religious dialectic overcomes the ultimate contradiction of history by effecting the casting off of history. There is a parallel between the individual, which we have been discussing, and history here. The ultimate antinomy present in the human being is necessarily present in history itself. Just as the individual cast off body-and-mind (Dōgen), history must ultimately cast itself off in order to be free of the abyss of absolute contradiction. Yet history is not thus considered superfluous or even as some sort of decline or corruption. The Formless Self realizes itself in wondrous, free activity, but does not remain confined to history. It is free to go in and out of history, now actualizing itself, now retreating to the root-source.

By way of moving in the direction of some sort of conclusion, we want to supplement what Hisamatsu means by time in order to better understand what he means by suprahistory and its relation to time. Strangely enough, he does not go into the problem of time in any detail, but seems to assume it as understood. Since this is an extremely difficult question, the extent to which we can "solve" it will be correspondingly limited, to say the least. But perhaps we will be able to throw some light on it.

> Religious time ought necessarily to be what coincides with historical time. I do not think that religious time is established in its relation to historical time by crossing the latter. I rather think that *historical time is established with religious time as its fundamental subject.* In other words, with Formless Self, or Self without form, as its basis and fundamental subject historical time is established. Therefore, the length dimension, as I mentioned above, comes to mean a Suprahistorical formation of history, a Suprahistorical living of history.[33]

By religious time crossing history, Hisamatsu means the traditional conception of transcendence and eternity as something above time that then intersects or vertically breaks into history. This conception he firmly rejects. We thus turn back to Nishitani, who did consider the question of time at some length. Taking the German term *Dasein* from Heidegger, Nishitani says that it can be considered under three forms.

> First, it is a *samskrta* (a being-at-doing) existence of infinite becoming within the world, coming to be and passing away from one fleeting moment to the next in time without beginning or end. It involves continually doing something.[34]

This infinity is what Nishitani calls "infinite finitude." Whether it is understood in Western terms as will or drive, or in Eastern terms as *karma*, we are incessantly driven to do something. This situation is essentially ambiguous. On the one hand, it implies creation, freedom, and infinite possibility; on the other hand, it shows the character of infinite burden and inextricable necessity. Sometimes we see this as a challenge and welcome it. At other times, we get overwhelmed by what must be done. Very little of what we do is done once and for all. For example, you cannot learn a language once and for all; you cannot learn to play a musical instrument once and for all; you can't even take a bath once and for all. This is infinite finitude.

What does Nishitani mean by "coming to be and passing away from one fleeting moment to the next in time without beginning or end?" Time without beginning or end we shall discuss presently. For now, Nishitani's statement means that we are living and dying at every instant. This is the Buddhist experiential "theory"[35] of instantaneity or momentariness. Time, instead of being a continuous flux, is radically discontinuous, coming into being and passing away each instant. This theory of time, while hardly acceptable to common sense, would probably make very good sense to most physicists. It is hard for us to gauge how the realization of this fact would profoundly alter our way of experiencing. Ueda Shizuteru points out that this is experienced to a certain degree in Zen meditation.

> Exhaling means continually departing from myself out into the infinite expanse of openness. Here already a dying takes place. Here already we may speak of a non-selfhood. Inhaling means drawing the infinite openness into oneself. Here already there is a resurrection.[36]

Hisamatsu states that man generally has two aspects to his experience, a sense of constancy and a sense of inconstancy. He needs them both. Without some feeling of constancy, without settling into some kind of present, he would find no ease. Without some feeling of inconstancy or change, he would tend to get bored. This was Schopenhauer's "insight" into human life, that it oscillates between the two poles of desire, wanting what it lacks, and, when it attains what it desired, boredom. But Schopenhauer got mired in his own affective reaction. It doesn't matter whether we like or dislike this state of affairs. The reaction to it blocks the real experience of it.

> It is wrong to consider ordinary things to be exclusively constant and "existent" (u), but it is also inappropriate to see them as being exclusively inconstant and "non-existent" (mu). Ordinary things are at once constant and inconstant, existent and non-existent. Because of his constancy, man has the capacity to feel always at ease; because of his inconstancy, man also feels anxious. However, anxiety pledges development into further constancy. Thus, the structure of ordinary things is one of constancy which is none other than inconstancy, unity which is none other than contradiction, being which is none other than non-being. Only in this way may we truly understand ordinary things.[37]

In this existential theory, the present does not follow the past horizontally in some kind of succession. Rather, the present flashes up vertically out of an infinite openness lying "beneath our feet," what Nishitani calls the "home-ground of the present." This is the dimension Nishitani means when he speaks of "time without beginning or end."

> Secondly, on the field of emptiness as absolute transcendence, a before is seen at the home-ground of the present that is before any past, however far back it be traced, and an after beyond any future capable of being projected. On this home-ground of the present, Dasein is eternal: Standing at the beginning, and hence also at the end, of time, it goes beyond time, beyond the world and its causality (the "three worlds"). This absolute transcendence, however, becomes manifest only in unison with the absolute immanence held up as the first form of Dasein.[38]

Here *Dasein* "breaks out of" time, that is, it breaks out of the conceptual overlay that it imposes on the sheer happening of instantaneity. The present does not follow the past in continuity; it arises out of the bottomless depth. That is why newness is possible: new ideas, new beginnings, new experiences. Why do we tend to get bored with what we have, whom we know, what we are doing? Because we fail to perceive this newness. Thus, we say that nothing lasts. Indeed nothing does last, not even for an instant. But we expect things to last horizontally, to persist throughout time. Even should we realize this vertical dimension of infinite openness, we would still to some extent continue to experience time horizontally. This is simply inevitable. Nishitani expresses this fact by stating that the second form of *Dasein*, that of transcendence, become manifest only in unison with the absolute immanence of the first form, that of immanence.

> Therefore, in the third place, in the same way that we can speak of birth *qua* unbirth, and extinction *qua* non-extinction, every instant of time can be called a "monad of eternity." Here each point of time throughout a past that reaches infinitely back into antiquity and each point of time in the infinite future ahead that lies further than we can see is likewise simultaneous with the present instant. The present instant only becomes manifest as something that projects (reflects) in itself, as it were, every sort of possible past and possible future. Alternatively, the present instant only becomes manifest as something into which are projected (transferred) all pasts from the beginning of time and all futures from the end of time. The instant comes about as a dharani maintaining all pasts and all futures in the home-ground of the present.[39]

The instant occurs as a dharani gathering all pasts and all futures, perhaps analogous to the manner in which for Heidegger the thing gathers the fourfold of earth, heaven, the godlike ones, and mortals. However, it is more difficult for most of us to think a *temporal* gathering. But perhaps not. At least we know that different times cannot impede each other.

> You must see all the various things of the whole world as so many times. These things do not get in each other's way any more than various times get in the way of each other.[40]

Night is night, and day is day. They do not get in each other's way. It is a well-established fact that in moments of grave danger people's whole lives flash before them in an instant. The *dharani* gathering all times to itself could help to elucidate this phenomenon.

> The idea of the present being simultaneous with every point in time past and future may sound rather farfetched at first. But if we bear in mind that the *beginning* of time is always in the present, and investigate the point thoroughly, we shall find such simultaneity to follow naturally as a matter of course.[41]

Time always begins, starts from the present. In the conception of time as a linear, irreversible flow, there is no possibility of a present, of a presence. What should we do to find this, interrupt the flow, stop it? How would this be accomplished? A conception of time that cannot account for a present is simply inadequate. After all, everyone has a sense of the present, however much they may obscure it by remembering the past or by anticipating the future. We seldom really are where we are. We need a conception of time that is *existential*, that belongs to someone's life. And the present must not be a "knife-edged," dimensionless present, but must in some sense include the dimensions of the past and future.

> But the true way of things is not to be found in this one direction alone. At the time the mountain was being

climbed and the river being crossed, I was there in time. The *time* has to <u>be</u> in me. Inasmuch as I am there, it cannot be that time passes away.[42]

The one direction alone in which the true way of things is not to be found is its quality of passing away, a quality that Dōgen does not deny, but feels that it is all that people see in time. In addition to the quality of passing by, and even that Dōgen understands differently from what most people think, Dōgen sees the crucial aspect of dwelling in a dharma-situation or a dharma-position.

> You reckon time only as something that does nothing but pass by, and do not understand it as something not yet arrived. Although our understandings are time, there is no chance for them to be drawn in by time. There has never been anyone who, while taking time to be coming and going, has penetrated to see it as a being-time dwelling in its dharma-position. What chance have you then for a time to break through the barrier to total emancipation? Even if there were someone who knew that dwelling-position, who would be able truly to give an utterance that preserved what he had thus gained? And even were someone able to give such utterance continually, he could still not help groping to bring his original face into immediate presence.[43]

Time is something not yet arrived (*mitō*). *Tō* is also translated a bit later on as "reaches." Waddell adds a footnote to the effect that *tō* can also mean "coming to fulfillment or attainment." Thus, *tō* seems to mean something like "getting there," and the statement that "you do not understand it as something not yet arrived" would appear to mean that there is a dimension of time that does not arrive in the present and pass away in a horizontal, linear fashion. In other words, there is an inexhaustible dimension to time. This is what Nishitani calls its "bottomlessness." Although the imagery is somewhat different, the thought is basically the same.

Even if one knows of that dwelling-situation, how can he possibly express it in such a way as to preserve it? And even if he were able to express this continually, which is unlikely, it still would not exhaust the matter at all and he would still have to grope to somehow bring his original face to immediate presence.

> For an instant is ever a present *now*; each point of time past and future, when it is constituted as time, can do so only in an instant. In this way, the present, while inexorably the present of time, is nonetheless simultaneous with each and every point of time past and future. The past never ceases to be *before* the present, and the future *after* the present; the order of before and after in temporal sequence is never abolished. That is, while each and every point of time is itself—the past inexorably as past, the future inexorably as future—they are also simultaneous with the present. In this simultaneity, the present encompasses all pasts and futures and maintains a collective hold [*dharani*] over them.[44]

How is such simultaneity possible? Obviously it is not possible if time is conceived as a horizontal, linear flow. It is possible only if the present is the originating source for the past and future and if at the base of the present there is an infinitely open bottomlessness.

> The infinite openness of time in both directions is nothing other than an introjection into time of the transtemporal openness or ecstatic transcendence lying directly beneath the present, and introjection achieved on each occasion of karmic activity.[45]

The transtemporal openness lying directly beneath the present is the source for the infinite horizontal openness in both directions of past and future. This occurs through karmic activity introjecting the depth dimension of that transtemporal openness onto a horizontal plane. At this point, the transtemporal openness that is reached and introjected onto a horizontal plane is encountered as nihility. The being of the self that comes about in that *karma* is at once voluntary and compulsory. That self is profoundly self-centered, caught, and trapped within itself, forever fated to transit endlessly through time in search of the homeground of the self. Nishitani compares this to Kierkegaard's sickness unto death, the many-faceted forms of despair that he so masterfully laid bare in the work of that name.

A further step is necessary, the step from the field of nihility to the field of emptiness and the corresponding move from the self-encapsulatedness of the self to the selfless, emptied self that can enter into "circuminsessional" interpenetration with all other things. "Circuminsessional" with its imagery of "circum," around, might tend to be a bit misleading. In fact, circuminsessional and interpenetration almost seem to contradict each other. Either things go "around" or else they go "into." Perhaps "circuminsessional," a term taken from speculation on the divine persons of the trinity, is not the best term to characterize this interpenetration ultimately having its roots in Hua-yen thought.

In this transparency and emptiness of the non-ego or true self, activity from one moment to the next originates from the beginning of time. In other words; each moment is a moment of eternity appearing in time.

In the conversion from the standpoint of *karma* to the standpoint of *śūnyatā*, *Dasein* achieves a true and elemental spontaneity, but this spontaneity is at once an earnestness in its elemental sense and a play in its elemental sense. Compared with that earnestness, the earnestness of any occupation on the standpoint of will prior to that conversion is mere time-killing divertissement, or *Zer-streuung*. However deep the concentration one invests in such occupation, to the extent that it is not performed in *samādhi*, the mind engaged in the doing is essentially distracted or "scattered."[46]

The "burden" imposed on us by our very existence, the fact that we are constantly driven to be doing something, and this doing constantly creates new *karma*, hence, the infinite need for more activity; this burden now ceases to be something imposed from outside of us as fate to something freely accepted as vocation or task. One might call this true "self-centeredness," a "gatheredness" keeping a collective hold (*dharani*) on all things. This is not the isolated self, cut off from the things of the world, but the self giving to all things their being.

Nishitani related the second form of *Dasein*, on the field of emptiness as absolute transcendence, to Nietzsche's philosophical position of the activity of the will on the field of atheistic nihility. Here time takes on the form of eternal recurrence. This time is reversible. Instead of a time without beginning or end, we have a time whose beginning and end are the same. Nothing new can come about. Eternity is perceived as eternal nihility. It has no contact whatever with history. This represents a mere dehistoricization of time. It is only with the third form, where every instant of time is a monad of eternity, that the true standpoint of emptiness is reached.

But however it be interpreted, so long as it includes the sense of a synthesis of time and eternity at the home-ground of the present, the horizon of simultaneity opens up there. On the horizon of eternity, things that are before and after within time are projected (reflected and transferred) into the home-ground of the present, even as the present is projected into the past and the future.[47]

Just as when forms one and two, absolute immanence and absolute transcendence, come together and the transtemporal openness lying directly beneath the present is projected on a horizontal plane as the infinite past and the infinite future, now that infinite past and infinite future are transferred back into the home-ground of the present. We have now reached the third form of *Dasein*, the intersection of time and eternity, and the possibility of a simultaneity of the whole of time in an instant. Nishitani says that the totality of time can only exist in a single instant. Otherwise, there is not possibility of a totality being "together," being all at once, that is, being a true totality.

> As the time right now is all there ever is, each being-time is without exception entire time. A being-grass and being-form are both times. Entire being, the entire world, exists in the time of each and every now. Just reflect: right now, is there an entire being or an entire world missing from your present time, or not?[48]

Nishitani calls the three forms of *Dasein* the "forms of illusion, emptiness, and the middle." The forms of illusion *(karma)* and emptiness *(śūnyatā)* should have become reasonably clear by now. What, then, does Nishitani mean here by "middle?" We have touched upon this before, but take it up now again briefly, since it is perhaps the most elusive of the three forms. Illusion and reality are familiar to us as categories. Again we ask, what is the "middle?" Once again Nishitani refers to samādhi.

> While the word refers in the first place to a mental state, it also applies to the mode of being of a thing in itself when it has settled into its own position. In that sense, we might call such a mode of being "samādhi-being." The form of things as they are on their own home-ground is similar to the appearance of things in samādhi. (To speak of the fact

that fire is burning, we could say that the fire is in its fire-samādhi).[49]

A thing in samādhi is a thing as it is on its own home-ground, not at all seen from the outside or represented.

It is not the case that we can just "get rid of" illusion once and for all. Illusion is there to stay. Only now we understand just what it is. It is illusory because it is one with emptiness. It is real because it is the *manifestation* of absolute selfhood. In the chapter on "The Personal and Impersonal in Religion," Nishitani discussed this in terms of the Tendai school of Buddhism, saying that man comes into being as the "middle" between "illusion" and "emptiness."

Ever trying to elucidate further the meaning of the middle, Nishitani states repeatedly that the field of *śūnyatā* has no circumference. Since we are accustomed to viewing things from the circumference, our "viewing" on the field of reason and the senses drops off. Thus, the center of this "circle" has no circumference; the center is everywhere.

But on a more essential level, a system of circuminsession has to be seen here, according to which, on the field of *śūnyatā*, all things are in a process of becoming master and servant to one another. In this system, each thing is itself in not being itself, and is not itself in being itself. Its being is illusion in its truth and truth in its illusion. This may sound strange the first time one hears it, but in fact it enables us for the first time to conceive of a *force* by virtue of which all things are gathered together and brought into relationship with one another, a force which, since ancient times, has gone by the name of "nature" (*physis*).[50]

Whereas Leibniz had simply stated, cryptically enough, that the monads reflected one another as living mirrors of the universe, Nishitani tried to *describe* this interpenetration of all things, a nearly impossible task. The field of *śūnyatā* is a field of force. This force enables things to interpenetrate, thus worlding world.

> In its being, we might say, the world "worlds." Such a mode of being is the mode of being of things as they are in themselves, their non-objective, "middle" mode of being as the selfness that they are.[51]

Speaking of the "natural light," Nishitani states that, contrary to Western thought, it is not the light of reason, but the light of each and every thing.

> The light that illumines us from our own home-ground and brings us back to an elemental self-awareness is but the nonobjective being of things as they are in themselves on the field where all things are manifest on their own home-ground.[52]

On this field all things settle into their own "position" or samādhi-being. Originally a term reserved for a kind of mental concentration, samādhi as Nishitani uses it is an *ontological* term designating the ultimate reality of all things.

By way of conclusion, we return to Hisamatsu for some final remarks on the Formless Self. After a section entitled "The Negative Clarification of Zen-Buddhist Nothingness" in which he once again lists what nothingness is not, Hisamatsu has a section entitled "The Positive Clarification of Zen-Buddhist Nothingness." Here he attempts to show that nothingness is not insentient or a blank lack of awareness. In the words of Hui-neng:

> The heart is so wide and great like the empty space of heaven; it is without limit and border.
>
> Your true nature is like the empty space of heaven, and when you are able to see the Not-something, this can be called right seeing.[53]

What is so difficult for us to grasp is the fact that this absolute nothingness is in no sense a *something*, and yet it is alive, active and has the characteristics of heart and self. Actually, we are not so inclined to think of heart or self as a some*thing*. They are to the extent "specific," as is also absolute nothingness, that one can say certain things about them. After all, the seven characteristics belonging to absolute nothingness and found inseparably in Zen art are definite characteristics. Whereas they remain somewhat vague as to "what" is being characterized, "moods" perhaps, but moods belonging more to what is being looked at than to someone looking at it, yet mood is perhaps not totally inappropriate here. "Mood" is related to "mode," way, and perhaps we can speak of the modes or ways of the Way. These moods or modes really do seem to belong to what is being depicted. Asymmetry, for example, is not a feeling aroused in someone looking at a painting. Yet these moods are not at all "subjective." We need another kind of "aesthetics" to be able to speak about this kind of Zen art. It really will absolutely not fit into a subject-object framework.

> In this kind of manifestation of Zen, I think there is something unique, something both extraordinary and artistic. When in the raising of a hand or in a single step something of Zen is present, that content seems to me to possess a very specific, artistic quality. A narrow conception of art might not accept that such manifestations contain anything artistic, but to me it seems that they possess an artistic quality that ordinarily cannot be seen. In fact, in such vital workings of Zen, I believe that something not merely artistic but also beyond art is involved, something toward which art should aim as its goal. Besides this concrete manifestative aspect, however, Zen also has an aspect that is "prior to form."
>
> This "prior to form" quality is far more basic than the concrete expressions of Zen activity, for only with the presence of the former is the activity given meaning.[54]

Zen activity, *Zenki*, is a term composed of two elements. *Zen* means whole, together, entire and *ki* means possibility, capacity, response, function, working. Thus, *Zenki* can mean entire working, an activity in which the whole is present with nothing left out.

Not unlike Nietzsche, Hisamatsu finds this undivided activity not in art proper alone, but in any activity of daily life, a gesture, the use of various utensils, the perception of aspects of nature. It is art moving in the direction of transcending itself, since it is form giving expression to what is prior to form, the formless. Nietzsche was close to this conception of art transcending itself when he characterized the world as a work of art giving birth to itself or when he thought of the artist as shaping himself and others. Yet the element of the formless was lacking in Nietzsche. And his conception of the Will to Power or of will in general is absolutely incompatible with what Hisamatsu is getting at.

What is of greatest significance in this literature, however, is not so much that it gives objective expression to Zen, as that Zen is present as a self-expressive, creative subject. In other words, that which is expressing itself and that which is expressed is identical.[55]

Awakening is thus not awakening *to* the self, but awakening *of* the self. The self is what awakens. This is, of course, not the ordinary self. The ordinary self is the body-mind that has dropped off. As long as we have not dropped off body and mind, there is absolutely no possibility for the Formless Self to awaken.

But Zen-Buddhist nothingness is by no means something unconscious and inanimate, as is emptiness, but it is the subject that knows itself "clearly and distinctly." Therefore one calls it "heart," "self," or " the true man."[56]

Following a genuine religious impulse, one is strongly inclined to take this Formless Self as a object of worship, as some-

thing "other" than myself. Whether Christian or Buddhist of the
Pure Land sect, one is strongly averse to setting oneself in the
place of "God." Of course, to consider my ego as god amounts to
the worst form of religious delusion or megalomania. That is
why the Great Death is absolutely essential. I must really let go
not only of my body with its demands, needs, and desires, but
above all of my insidiously grasping mind with its obsessions,
fixations, and delusions. The Buddha found this out when his attempts at asceticism got him nowhere. However much we may
weaken and enfeeble the body, the incessantly clinging mind
remains.

To get a sense of what it means that Buddha or the Formless
Self is to be sought nowhere outside of oneself, that we nevertheless have no conception of what that Formless Self is, we return in
conclusion to the thinker with whom we began, to Dōgen. This
fact of having no conception, no inkling of what the Formless Self
is, even though it can be found nowhere outside of us, is most
likely the reason why we do search outside of ourselves. We think
that we can know ourselves, and that this cannot be "it."

> Buddha-dharma cannot be known by a person. For this
> reason, since olden times no ordinary person has realized
> Buddha-dharma; no practitioner of the Lesser Vehicles
> has mastered Buddha-dharma. Because it is realized by
> buddhas alone, it is said, "only a buddha and a buddha
> can thoroughly master it."
>
> When you realize Buddha-dharma, you do not think
> "this is realization just as I expected." Even if you think
> so, realization invariably differs from your expectation.
> Realization is not like your conception of it. Accordingly,
> realization cannot take place as previously conceived.
> When you realize Buddha-dharma, you do not consider
> how realization came about. You should reflect on this.
> What you think one way or another before realization is
> not a help for realization.[57]

This reminds us of the kōan about the person sitting in order to become a Buddha. Someone picked up a tile and began polishing it. When asked what he was doing, the tile-polisher answered that he was trying to make a mirror out of the tile. The person sitting said it was impossible to turn a tile into a mirror. Similarly, no amount of sitting can turn an ordinary person into a Buddha. And yet there have been Buddhas, persons who have attained realization.

Only a Buddha can become a Buddha; an ordinary person cannot do so. Yet Dōgen tells us that all sentient beings are the Buddha-nature. They do not *have* it; they *are* it. This was the quandary that set Dōgen out on his search for an "answer" to the question: if we are already the Buddha-nature, why is it necessary to practice?

Realization absolutely cannot be anticipated. When you realize Buddha-dharma, you do not think, "This is realization just as I expected."[58] Even if you think so, realization invariably differs from your expectation.

This passage, which we cited before, is crucial. Actually, it is difficult for us to really anticipate anything. Ordinary, everyday occurrences and activities can be more or less anticipated, but generally I take them so much for granted that I take them as a matter of course without bothering to anticipate them to any appreciable degree. It is otherwise with something with which I am affectively involved. I may dread something. It weighs on me as a burden, and is all I can think about, for instance, an examination, an operation, an important appointment. But even this dread often turns out to have little to do with what actually happens. What happens may not be bad at all, or it may be just terrible. The case is similar when I look forward to something. The Germans have a word for this, *Vorfreude*, the joy before. This can be a wonderful feeling, unmarred by any reality. When the event actually occurs, it may be totally insignificant. At any rate, it, too, soon passes.

Although realization is not like any of the thoughts preceding it, this is not because such thoughts were actually bad and could not be realization. Past thoughts were already realization. But since you were seeking elsewhere, you thought and said that thoughts cannot be realization.

However, it is worth noticing that what you think one way or another is not a help for realization. Then you are cautious not to be small-minded. If realization came forth by the power of your prior thoughts, it would not be trustworthy. Realization does not depend on thoughts, but comes forth far beyond them; realization is helped only by the power of realization itself. Know that then there is no delusion, and there is no realization.[59]

Here Dōgen states that the past thoughts preceding realization were already realization. This is in accord with his conviction that all beings are the Buddha-nature. But the point is that we were seeking, looking for and anticipating something elsewhere. The key statement here is that realization does not depend on thoughts. Whatever it is, realization is not thoughts. We do not *think* realization. We ask immediately: what else can it be? But we cannot ask in this way. Realization comes forth far beyond thoughts. Awakening, or realization, is not a thought. I can only realize something that is already there.

The questions centering around the "before" and "after" enlightenment are to an extent crystallized in the controversy over original and acquired enlightenment. Dōgen states conclusively that all beings are, not have, the Buddha-nature. But if they do not *realize* this, it is useless. We are immediately confronted with a mass of aporias. But we must work through them, since this is the only way we have to get beyond conceptualizing.

We already are the Buddha-nature. Although this statement is "true," the implications which it suggests are not. So conceived, the Buddha-nature is something static in all of us, a view bordering on eternalism.

On the other hand, polishing a tile in order to make a mirror or sitting in order to become a Buddha is not possible. The tile is already a mirror, sitting itself is already being a Buddha. But tile-polishing and sitting are crucial. The hitch lies in stating that the title *becomes* the mirror, the sitter *becomes* a Buddha. We cannot say this, no matter how strongly common sense dictates that we should.

We should not isolate and absolutize this question, but consider it in the context of Dōgen's thought as a whole. The idea of becoming, so familiar to us all, is denied by Dōgen. Just as winter does not become spring, firewood does not become ash, birth does not become death, an ignorant person does not become or turn into a Buddha. This is also the reason why Dōgen will consistently change a construction traditionally read as "If *x* happens in the future or you should do *x*" to read "*x* is happening right now."

> By way of illustration, *if you wish to know the Buddha-nature's meaning* might be read, "you are directly knowing the Buddha-nature's meaning." *You should watch for temporal conditions* means "you are directly knowing temporal conditions." If you wish to know the Buddha-nature, you should know that it is precisely temporal conditions themselves.
>
> The utterance *If the time arrives* means "The time is already here, and there could be no room to doubt it.[60]

In the fascicle entitled "Awakening the Buddha-seeking Mind" Dōgen delves further into the question of how this "transition," which is no transition, is possible. He distinguishes three kinds of mind: *citta*, the discriminating mind; *karit*, the mind of grass and trees; and *irita*, the mind of truth. *Karit*, the mind of grass and trees, is "innocent," it does not discriminate; nor can it become anything other than what it is. It is *citta*, the discriminating mind, which can awaken to the Buddha-seeking mind. It is not the same as the Buddha-seeking mind, but we cannot awaken to the Buddha-seeking mind without it. The Buddha-seeking mind is not innate nor does it arise through recent experience, neither is it singular nor plural, definable or indefinable, within ourselves or universal. It bears no relation to the future or past, and neither can we say it "is" or "isn't," nor is it the essence of ourselves, others, or both, nor does it suddenly occur, but it arises as the gradual result of a spiritual link between ourselves and the Buddha. This mind cannot be transmitted by the Buddhas and Bodhisattvas nor can it be induced through our own efforts. Only a spiritual link between ourselves and the Buddha can awaken the Buddha-seeking mind.[61]

Dōgen almost outdoes Nagarjuna in the kinds of statements one cannot make about the Buddha-seeking mind. He comes up with a sort of Omnilemma; The Buddha-seeking mind is not innate; we do not already have it. Nor does it arise through our experience, past or future; we cannot acquire it. It is the result of a spiritual link between ourselves and the Buddha. This does not tell us very much. But Dōgen elaborates a little on this when he states several times that we should undertake to assist all sentient beings to attain enlightenment before we consider our own. When we do this, the discriminating mind turns into the Buddha-seeking mind.

When we awaken the Buddha-seeking mind, even if only for a moment, all things become conducive to its growth. Awakening the Buddha-seeking mind and experiencing enlightenment may occur and perish momentarily. If this were not so momentary past wrongs could not disappear and subsequent good could not appear. The Tathāgata alone understands this fully, for it is only he who can utter an entire word in an instant.[62]

This idea of the possibility of past wrongs being able to disappear ("forgiveness of sins," repentance) is later in the twentieth century developed by Tanabe as *zange* or metanoetics (mind-conversion).

> With the passing of each instant we undergo the incessant action of existing and non-existing. In the time it takes an average middle-aged man to "click" his fingers, sixty-five such instants pass, and over the space of twenty-four hours, 6,400,099,980 take place. The ordinary person, totally unaware of these facts, in unable to awaken the Buddha-seeking mind.[63]

What is meant here by "instant" by no means coincides with our ordinary conception of it. The radicality of this conception of impermanence is scarcely conceivable to most of us. Dōgen repeats the exact same "fantastical" (in Kierkegaard's sense of that word) numbers in a fascicle entitled "Shukke Kudoku," "The Virtue of Renouncing the World," and states there that although there are many enlightened people, only Shakyamuni and Sariputtra were able to realize the change which occurs in one instant.[64] But it is precisely through this constant activity of death and rebirth, this incredible "dynamicity" of impermanence, that awakening to enlightenment is possible. In a continuity of static persistence, there is no "room," no occasion, no *kairos* for anything to happen.

We have again and again returned our focus to the question of time. It remains in conclusion to try to clarify the relation of the self to time and, finally, to ask in what sense the Formless Self is a self. Broaching the question of how the self came historically to be related to time in Western philosophy, we can perhaps begin with Kant who moved the focus on time away from the realm of nature and the concomitant emphasis on time measurement. Actually, he did not move it away from the realm of nature, but redefined "nature" as the totality of appearances (*Inbegriff der Erscheinungen*). Thus, time becomes the form of inner sensibility, the form of our awareness of all internal experience and indirectly the form of all experience whatsoever. When he states that the "I think" must be able to accompany all consciousness, he established the definitive link between time and consciousness without specifying just what the nature of this "accompanying" was. It was Husserl who in the lectures entitled "The Phenomenology of Internal Time Consciousness" gave phenomenological descriptions of time not as the form of consciousness, but as the actual occurrence of consciousness. These lectures were edited by Heidegger who then went on to establish the link between time and being. The question of the meaning of being thus usurped the place of the question of the self which then never became and never could become a separate issue for him. Human being was being-there (*Da-sein*), replaced in the later thought by the term "mortals."

In Buddhism, there is no alignment of the self with time nor can the self be considered as a separate entity. Self is no-self (*anatman, muga*). Thus, neither time nor the self mean what they do in Western thought. In modern Western thought, both in literature as well as in philosophy, the concept of a stream of consciousness comes roughly to stand for both time and the self. If time is not conceived objectively as time measurement, as clock time, it moves closer to our subjective, psychological "sense" of time. Buddhism has no such bifurcation of the subjective and the objective. Thus, time cannot be thought in those terms either. Nor can the self, strange as that may sound. The self is nothing subjective. How is such an outrageous assertion possible?

Because it is fundamentally no-thing, the self may be said to be the boundless possibility to become all things. Human being is this possibility to an eminent degree.

> We set the self out in array and make that the whole world. You must see all the various things of the whole world as so many times.[65]

What does it mean, to set the self out in array? The self has no form; it is no-thing. Thus, it is intrinsically capable of *ecstasis*, of getting outside itself, of opening itself out to become all things. This is the dead opposite of re-flection, of bending back into itself and so encapsulating itself. This is also ultimately the fundamental meaning of exertion and also of impeding. I cannot exert anything but myself. And Dōgen states that a thing only impedes itself, never anything else.

> Reaching is impeded by reaching and is not impeded by not-reaching. Not-reaching is impeded by not-reaching and is not impeded by reaching. Mind impedes mind and sees mind, word impedes word and sees word, impeding impedes itself and sees itself. Impeding impedes impeding—that is time.[66]

When a thing impedes itself, it takes a form and becomes manifest. Before it took on form, it was formless. Formlessness or emptiness can only become manifest in unison with form. Time is, so to speak, the dynamic "functioning" of emptiness, its power of articulating itself into form.

On a Portrait of Myself

Cold lake, for thousands of yards, soaks up sky color.
Evening quiet: a fish of brocade scales reaches bottom, then goes
    first this way, then that way; arrow notch splits.
Endless waters surface moonlight brilliant.[67]

Conclusion

With regard to the question in what sense a Formless Self can be a self, we would in conclusion be able to reply that if selfhood is not to be conceived egotistically as a separate self opposed and hostile to everything other than itself, formlessness offers an eminent possibility of rethinking selfhood. Overcoming and abandoning its anxious sense of itself as an encapsulated separate "I," the self gains the wondrous freedom and openness to emerge in joyous compassion from the shackles of its self-imposed boundaries.

$\widehat{Notes}$

Chapter 1: *Dōgen*

1. Hee-Jin Kim, *Flowers of Emptiness*, (Lewiston, NY: The Edwin Mellen Press, 1985).

2. D. T. Suzuki, *The Essence of Buddhism* (Kyoto: Bunko, 1948), p. 65.

3. Ludwig Wittgenstein, *Traktatus Logico-Philosophicus* (London: Routledge & Kegan Paul, 1958), p. 150.

4. Wittgenstein, *Traktatus*, p. 56.

5. *Ibid.*, p. 51.

6. *Ibid.*

7. *Dōgen Kigen, Mystical Realist* (Tucson: University of Arizona Press, 1975), p. 221.

8. Kim, *Flowers of Emptiness*, p. 197.

9. Francis Cook, *How to Raise an Ox* (Los Angeles, CA: Center Publications, 1978), p. 55.

10. Kim, *Flowers of Emptiness*, p. 201.

11. *Muchu-setsumu (Dreams within Dreams)*, quoted in Kim, *Mystical Realist*, p. 113.

12. *Ibid.*, p. 273.

13. *Ibid.*, p. 276.

14. Kazuaki Tanahashi, ed., *Moon in a Dewdrop* (San Francisco: North Point Press, 1985), p. 162. "Only Buddha and Buddha" (Yuibutsu Yobutsu).

15. *Ibid.*

16. *Ibid.*

17. *Ibid.*, p. 164.

18. *Ibid.*

19. *Ibid.*, p. 167.

20. Norman Waddell and Abe Masao, trans., "Buddha-nature," *The Eastern Buddhist* 8, no. 2:100–1.

21. *Ibid.*, p. 101.

22. *Ibid.*

23. *Ibid.*, p. 108.

24. *Ibid.*, pp. 111–12.

25. *Philosophical Studies of Japan*, vol. Ii, 1960, p. 93.

26. *Eastern Buddhist*, 10, no. 1:10.

27. *Ibid.*, p. 12.

28. "Buddha-nature," *Eastern Buddhist*, 9, no. 1:90.

29. *Eastern Buddhist*, 7, no. 2:100.

30. *Ibid.*, pp. 102–4.

31. *Ibid.*, p. 105.

32. *Ibid.*, p. 91.

33. *Ibid.*, p. 104.

34. "Uji," *Eastern Buddhist*, 12, no. 1:116.

35. Kim, "Uji," in *Flowers of Emptiness* (see n. 1 above), p. 229.

36. Norman Waddell and Abe Masao, trans., "Genjō-kōan," *Eastern Buddhist* 5, no. 2:134–35.

37. *Ibid.*, p. 125.

38. *Ibid.*, p. 136.

39. Discussed in "Koky," (The Primordial Mirror) (Tokyo: Nakayama, 1983), vol. 3, p. 45.

40. *Ibid.*, p. 38.

41. As a college student, I was assigned to read Levy-Bruhl. When I read that for primitive man everything was alive, my first thought was: one could never be alone.

42. Tanahashi, ed., "Mountains and Waters Sutra," in *Moon in a Dewdrop*, pp. 97–8.

43. Tanahashi, ed., "Only Buddha knows Buddha," in *Moon in a Dewdrop*, p. 161.

44. *Ibid.*, pp. 151–52.

45. *Ibid.*, p. 162.

46. Wünschbarkeiten.

47. *Ibid.*

48. *Ibid.*

49. *Ibid.*, p. 167.

Chapter 2: *Hisamatsu*

1. *Eastern Buddhist* 4, no. 2:94.

2. Dōgen, "Admonitions for Zazen" (Zazenshin), in Hee-Jin Kim, *Flowers of Emptiness*, p. 157.

3. *Ibid.*, p. 98.

4. Meister Eckhart, *Sermons and Treatises*, vol. 2, M. O'C. Walshe trans. (Dorset: Element Books, 1987), p. 273.

5. *Ibid.*, pp. 273–74.

6. *Ibid.*, p. 99.

7. *Julius Caesar* (New York: Macmillan, 1949).

8. Richard De Martino, interpreter, *Eastern Buddhist* 5, no. 2:110.

9. *Ibid.*, p. 119.

10. *Ibid.*, p. 120.

11. Martino, *Eastern Buddhist* 6, no. 2:89.

12. *Ibid.*, p. 95.

13. *Ibid.*, p. 99.

14. *Ibid.*, p. 102.

15. *Ibid.*, p. 108.

16. *Ibid.*, p. 111.

17. Kant, *Critique of Pure Reason*, Norman Kemp Smith, trans. (New York: St. Martin's Press, 1965), p. 295.

18. *Ibid.*, p. 93.

19. Hisamatsu, "The Characteristics of Oriental Nothingness," in *Philosophical Studies of Japan* Ii (1960):67.

20. *Ibid.*, p. 32.

21. Wilson Van Dusen, "The Mystery of Ordinary Experiencing," in *The Meeting of the Ways* (New York: Schocken Books, 1979), p. 68.

22. Hisamatsu, *Oriental Nothingness*, p. 83.

23. *Ibid.*, p. 87.

24. Kogetsu Tani and Eido Tai Shimano, *Zen Wort Zen Schrift* (Zürich: Theseus Verlag, 1990), p. 156.

25. Hoseki Shin'ichi Hisamatsu, *Die Fülle des Nichts*, Takashi Hirata and Johanna Fischer, trans. (Pfullingen: Neske Verlag, 1984), p. 19.

26. 80 d. *Phaedo* (Plato)

27. Hisamatsu, *Die Fülle des Nichts*, p. 40.

28. *Ibid.*, p. 41.

29. Shin'ichi Hisamatsu, *Zen and the Fine Arts* (New York: Kodansha International, 1974), p. 19.

30. *Ibid.*, p. 30.

31. *Ethics II*, def. 6; IV, Preface.

32. Hisamatsu, *Zen and the Fine Arts*, p. 31.

33. *Ibid.*, p. 45.

34. *Ibid.*, p. 48.

35. *Ibid.*, p. 49.

36. *Ibid.*, pp. 49–50.

37. *Ibid.*, p. 51.

38. *Ibid.*

39. Toshihiko Izutsu, *Toward a Philosophy of Zen Buddhism* (Boulder, CO: 1982), p. 153.

40. Kim, *Flowers of Emptiness*, p. 298.

41. *Ibid.*, p. 299.

42. Izutsu, *Philosophy of Zen*, p. 141.

43. *Ibid.*, p. 171.

44. *Ibid.*, p. 131.

45. *Ibid.*, p. 212.

46. John Welwood and Ken Wilber, "On Ego Strength and Egolessness," in *The Meeting of the Ways* (New York: Schocken Books, 1979), p. 109.

47. *Ibid.*

48. Quoted in John Welwood, "Meditation and the Unconscious," in *The Meeting of the Ways*, p. 15.

49. *Ibid.*, p. 151.

50. *Ibid.*, p. 160.

52. Smith, trans., *Critique of Pure Reason*, B316, A 262.

53. Welwood, *The Meeting of the Ways*, p. 169.

Chapter 3: *Nishitani*

1. Nishitani, *The Self-Overcoming of Nihilism*, trans. Graham Parkes with Setsuko Aihara (Albany: State University of New York Press, 1990), p. 1.

2. *Ibid.*, p. 3.

3. Traceable back to Indian thought, mappō is the last and worst in the series of world epochs.

4. *Ibid.*, p. 97.

5. Nishitani, *Religion and Nothingness*, Jan. Van Bragt, trans. (Berkeley: University of California, 1982), p. 4.

6. Nishitani, *Nishida-Kitaro*, Yanamoto Seisaka and James W. Heisig, trans. (Berkeley: University of California, 1991), p. 112.

7. *Ibid.*, p. 114.

8. *Ennead VI*, 4, Loeb Library, vol. 7, p. 317.

9. Nishitani, *Religion and Nothingness* (see ch. 3, n. 5), p. 154.

10. *Ibid.*, p. 155.

11. Nishitani, *Nishida Kitarō*, p. 102.

12. *Eastern Buddhist* 5, no. 2:133.

13. Nishitani, *Religion and Nothingness*, pp. 199–200.

14. Paul Tillich, *The Courage To Be* (New Haven: Yale University Press), 1959.

15. Nishitani, *Religion and Nothingness* (see ch. 3, n. 5), p. 216.

16. *Eastern Buddhist* 25, no. 1:61–62.

17. Nishitani, *Religion and Nothingness*, p. 129.

18. *Ibid.*, p. 130.

19. *Ibid.*, p. 164.

20. Hisamatsu, *Zen and the Fine Arts*, p. 51.

21. *Eastern Buddhist* 15, no. 1:22.

22. Hisamatsu, "Ultimate Crisis and Resurrection," in *Eastern Buddhist* 8, no. 1:21–22.

23. Hisamatsu, "Zen: Its Meaning for Modern Civilization," in *Eastern Buddhist* 1, no. 1:32.

24. *Eastern Buddhist* 8, no. 1:14.

25. *Eastern Buddhist* 8, no. 2:50.

26. *Eastern Buddhist* 8, no. 2:52.

27. *Ibid.*

28. *Eastern Buddhist, ibid.*, p. 40.

29. *Eastern Buddhist* 8, no. 2:14.

30. *Eastern Buddhist* 8, no. 2:64.

31. *Eastern Buddhist* 12, no. 1:4.

32. *Eastern Buddhist* 12, no. 1:5.

33. *Eastern Buddhist* 8, no. i:14.

34. Nishitani, *Religion and Nothingness*(see ch. 3, n. 5), p. 266.

35. Theory in the sense of "therein to see."

36. *Eastern Buddhist* 16, no. 1:55.

37. *Eastern Buddhist* 12, no. 1:4–5.

38. Nishitani, *Religion and Nothingness*, p. 266.

39. *Ibid.*

40. Dōgen, "Uji," *Eastern Buddhist* 12, no. 1:117.

41. Nishitani, *Religion and Nothingness*, p. 267.

42. Dōgen, "Uji," p. 119.

43. *Ibid.*, p. 123.

44. Nishitani, *Religion and Nothingness*, pp. 266–67.

45. *Ibid.*, p. 245.

46. *Religion and Nothingness*, p. 259.

47. *Ibid.*, p. 269.

48. Dōgen, "Uji," p. 118.

49. Nishitani, *Religion and Nothingness* (see ch. 3, n. 5), p. 128.

50. *Ibid.*, p. 149.

51. *Ibid.*, p. 150.

52. *Ibid.*, p. 164.

53. *Ibid.*

54. Hisamatsu, *Zen and the Fine Arts*, p. 12.

55. *Ibid.*, p. 16.

56. Hisamatsu, *Die Fülle des Nichts*, p. 34.

57. Tanahashi, "Only Buddha and Buddha," p. 161.

58. *Ibid.*

59. *Ibid.*, pp. 161–62.

60. *Eastern Buddhist* 8, no. 2:104.

61. Nishiyama et al., trans., *Shōbōgenzō*, vol. III (Tokyo: Nakayama, 1983), p. 89.

62. *Ibid.*, p. 91.

63. *Ibid.*

64. *Ibid.*, p. 91.

65. Dōgen, "Uji," p. 117.

66. *Ibid.*

67. Tanahashi, ed., *Moon in a Dewdrop*, p. 127.

Index

nikon, 10, 32, 34
nirvana, 36
Nishida, Kitaro, 108–111
no-mind, 55–7, 92, 96–7

ox-herding pictures, 21, 129

person, 17, 113, 153
Plato, 18, 30, 40, 79, 100, 109,
 118–140
Plotinus, 35, 109
Pure Land, 81, 133, 157

Sakyamuni, 130, 162
Sartre, Jean-Paul, 2, 47, 49
satori, 85
Schelling, F.W., 64, 120
Schopenhauer, Arthur, 120
Shakespeare, 62
shinjindatsuraku, 2, 6

skandhas, 18, 51
Socrates, 15
Spinoza, 81
suchness, 4, 18, 81–2
Suzuki, D.T., 2, 126

Tanabe, Hajime, 162
Taoism, Taoist, 4, 126
temporality, 28

Ueda, Shizuteru, 126, 129
uji, 8, 12, 17, 31
Upanishads, 20

Waddell, Norman, 148
Wittgenstein, 2
wu wei, 4

Zenki, 5, 7, 9, 156